WORLD WIDE WEB

WORLD WIDE WEB

Mahendra Kumar Goel

RAJAT PUBLICATIONS
Publishers & Distributors
NEW DELHI - 110 002

WORLD WIDE WEB

This edition is published by Rajat Publications
4740/23, Ansari Road Daryaganj,
New Delhi - 110002

ISBN: 978-81-7880-487-3

Edition 2026

Printed and bound in India

RAJAT
PUBLICATIONS

4740/23, Ansari Road, Daryaganj,
New Delhi- 110002 (India)
Tel:- +91-11-23267924
Mob:- +91-9811484973, +91-9811105389
E-mail: rajat_publication@yahoo.com

Preface

The World Wide Web (WWW) is a system of inter-linked hyper-text documents accessed via the internet. With a web browser, one can view web pages that may contain text, images, videos, and other multimedia and navigate between them using hyperlinks. The web was developed to be a pool of human knowledge, which would allow collaborators in remote sites to share their ideas and all aspects of a common project.

The web began as a networked information project at CERN, where Tim Berners-Lee, now Director of the World Wide Web Consortium (W3C), developed a vision of the project. The web has a body of software, and a set of protocols and conventions. Through the use hyper-text and multimedia techniques, the web is easy for anyone to roam, browse, and contribute to. Now, the web has matured into a powerful tool for scientists, engineers, and researchers. Far more than a collection of hot links and cool sites, today's web represents a sea change in our professional lives, providing new ways to communicate ideas and information.

The present book is a treasure trove of authentic information on the development and functioning of World Wide Web. For internet and web users in the scientific and engineering community, this book provides strategies and essential information to help you move beyond simply browsing the web.

Mahendra Kumar Goel

Contents

1

Intrdocuction

The World Wide Web is a system of interlinked, hypertext documents accessed via the Internet. With a web browser, a user views web pages that may contain text, images, videos, and other multimedia and navigates between them using hyperlinks. The World Wide Web was created in 1989 by Sir Tim Berners-Lee from the United Kingdom, and Robert Cailliau from Belgium, working at CERN in Geneva, Switzerland. Since then, Berners-Lee has played an active role in guiding the development of web standards (such as the markup languages in which web pages are composed), and in recent years has advocated his vision of a Semantic Web.

Viewing a web page on the World Wide Web normally begins either by typing the URL of the page into a web browser, or by following a hypertext link to that page or resource. The first step, behind the scenes, is for the server-name part of the URL to be resolved into an IP address by the global, distributed Internet database known as the domain name system, or DNS.

The browser then requests the resource by sending an HTTP request to the web server at that IP address. In the case of a typical web page, the HTML text is requested first and parsed by the browser, which then makes additional requests for graphics and any other files that form a part of the page in quick succession. When considering website popularity statistics, these additional file requests give rise to the difference between a single 'page view' and an associated number of server 'hits'.

The web browser then renders the page as described by the HTML, CSS, and other files received, incorporating the images and other resources as necessary. This produces the on-screen page that the viewer sees. Most web pages will themselves contain hyperlinks to other related pages and perhaps to downloads, source documents, definitions and other web resources. Such a collection of useful, related resources, interconnected via hypertext links, is what has been dubbed a "web" of information. Making it available on the Internet created what Tim Berners-Lee first called the WorldWideWeb in 1990.

Web Standards

Web standards is a general term for the formal standards and other technical specifications that define and describe aspects of the World Wide Web. In recent years, the term has been more frequently associated with the trend of endorsing a set of standardized best practices for building web sites, and a philosophy of web design and development that includes those methods.

Many interdependent standards and specifications, some of which govern aspects of the Internet, not just the World Wide Web, directly or indirectly affect the development and administration of web sites and web services. While any of these may be called "web standards," advocates within the web standards movement tend to focus on the higher-level standards that most directly affect the accessibility and usability of web sites. Web standards, in the broader sense, consist of the following:

- — Recommendations published by the World Wide Web Consortium (W3C)
- — Internet standard (STD) documents published by the Internet Engineering Task Force (IETF)
- — Request for Comments (RFC) documents published by the Internet Engineering Task Force
- — Standards published by the International Organization for Standardization (ISO)
- — Standards published by Ecma International (formerly ECMA)
- — The Unicode Standard and various Unicode Technical Reports (UTRs) published by the Unicode Consortium
- — Name and number registries maintained by the Internet Assigned Numbers Authority (IANA)

Usually, when a Web site or Web page is described as complying with Web standards, it means the site or page has HTML that is semantic and valid or nearly valid, along with valid or nearly valid CSS.

Also, when Web standards are discussed, the following publications are typically seen as foundational:

- — Recommendations for markup languages, such as HTML, XHTML, SVG, and XForms, from W3C.
- — Recommendations for stylesheets, especially CSS, from W3C.
- — Standards for ECMAScript, a.k.a. JavaScript, from Ecma International.
- — Recommendations for the Document Object Model, from W3C.

A W3C Recommendation is a specification or set of guidelines that, after extensive consensus-building, has received the endorsement of W3C Members and the Director.An IETF Internet Standard is characterized by a high degree of technical maturity and by a generally held belief that the specified protocol or service provides significant benefit to the Internet community.A specification that reaches the status of Standard is assigned a number in the IETF STD series while retaining its original IETF RFC number.

World Wide Web Consortium (W3C)

The World Wide Web Consortium (W3C) is the main international standards organization for the World Wide Web (W3). It is arranged as a consortium where member organizations maintain full-time staff for the purpose of working together in the development of standards for the W3. As of March 2007, the W3C had 441 members. It is always open for new organizations to join.

W3C also engages in education and outreach, develops software and serves as an open forum for discussion about the Web.

The Consortium is headed by Sir Tim Berners-Lee, the primary author of the original URL (Uniform Resource Locator), HTTP (HyperText Transfer Protocol) and HTML (HyperText Markup Language) specifications, the principal technologies that form the basis of the World Wide Web.

Tim Berners-Lee left the European Organization for Nuclear Research (CERN) in October, 1991 and founded the World Wide Web Consortium (W3C) at the Massachusetts Institute of Technology Laboratory for Computer Science (MIT/LCS) with support from the Defense Advanced Research Projects Agency (DARPA) — which had pioneered the Internet — and the European Commission.

The consortium was created to ensure compatibility and agreement among industry members in the adoption of new standards. Prior to its creation, incompatible versions of HTML were offered by different vendors, increasing the potential for inconsistency between web pages. The consortium was created to get all those vendors to agree on a set of core principles and components which would be supported by everyone.

It was originally intended that CERN host the European branch of W3C. However, CERN wished to focus on particle physics, not information technology. In April 1995 the Institut national de recherche en informatique et en automatique (INRIA) became the European host of W3C, with Keio University becoming the Japanese branch in September 1996. Starting in 1997, W3C created regional offices around the world; as of May 2006 it has sixteen World Offices covering Australia, the Benelux countries (the Netherlands, Luxemburg, and Belgium), Mainland China, Finland, Germany and Austria, Greece, Hong Kong, Hungary, India, Ireland, Israel, Italy, Japan, South Korea, Korea, Morocco, Spain, Sweden, the United Kingdom and the United States.

In January 2003, the European host was transferred from INRIA to the European Research Consortium for Informatics and Mathematics (ERCIM), an organization that represents European national computer science laboratories.

In accord with the W3C Process Document, a Recommendation progresses through five maturity levels:

— Working Draft (WD)

— Last Call Working Draft

— Candidate Recommendation (CR)

— Proposed Recommendation (PR)

— W3C Recommendation (REC)

A Recommendation may be updated by separately published Errata until enough substantial edits accumulate, at which time a new edition of the Recommendation may be produced (e.g., XML is now in its fourth edition). W3C also publishes various kinds of informative Notes which are not intended to be treated as standards.

The Consortium leaves it up to manufacturers to follow the Recommendations. Many of its standards define levels of conformance, which the developers must follow if they wish to label their product W3C-compliant. Like any standards of other organizations, W3C recommendations are sometimes implemented partially. The Recommendations are under a royalty-free patent license, allowing anyone to implement them.

Unlike the ISOC and other international standards bodies, the W3C does not have a certification program. A certification program is a process which has benefits and drawbacks; the W3C has decided, for now, that it is not suitable to start such a program owing to the risk of creating more drawbacks for the community than benefits.

The Consortium is jointly administered by the MIT Computer Science and Artificial Intelligence Laboratory (CSAIL) in the USA, the European Research Consortium for Informatics and Mathematics (ERCIM) (in Sophia Antipolis, France), and Keio University (in Japan). The W3C also has World Offices in fifteen regions around the world. The W3C Offices work with their regional Web communities to promote W3C technologies in local languages, broaden W3C's geographical base, and encourage international participation in W3C Activities.

CACHING

If a user revisits a web page after only a short interval, the page data may not need to be re-obtained from the source web server. Almost all web browsers cache recently-obtained data, usually on the local hard drive. HTTP requests sent by a browser will usually only ask for data that has changed since the last download. If the locally-cached data is still current, it will be reused.

Caching helps reduce the amount of web traffic on the Internet. The decision about expiration can be made independently for each downloaded file, whether image, stylesheet, JavaScript, HTML, or whatever other content the site may provide. Thus even on sites with highly dynamic content, many of the basic resources may only need to be refreshed once every few sessions. Web site designers may find it worthwhile to collate shared resources such as CSS data and JavaScript into a few site-wide files so that they can be cached efficiently. This helps reduce page download times and lowers demands on the web server.

There are other components of the Internet that can also cache web content. In practice, the most widely-used caches are built into corporate and academic firewalls which cache web resources requested by one user for the benefit of all. Some search engines, such as Google or Yahoo!, also store cached content from web sites. Apart from the facilities built into web servers that can determine when files have been updated, designers of dynamically-generated web pages can control the HTTP headers sent back to requesting users, so that transient or sensitive pages are not cached. Internet banking and news sites frequently use these facilities.

This helps with understanding the difference between the HTTP "GET" and "POST" commands: data requested with a GET is likely to be cached, if other conditions are met, whereas data obtained via a POST command will be assumed to be transient and will not be cached.

JAVA AND JAVASCRIPT

A significant advance in Web technology was Sun Microsystems' Java platform. It enables web pages to embed small programs (called applets) directly into the view. These applets run on the end-user's computer, providing a richer user interface than simple web pages. Java client-side applets never gained the popularity that Sun had hoped for a variety of reasons, including lack of integration with other content and the fact that many computers at the time were supplied to end users without a suitably installed Java Virtual Machine, and so required a download by the user before applets would appear. Adobe Flash now performs many of the functions that were originally envisioned for Java applets, including the playing of video content, animation, and some rich UI features. Java itself has become more widely used as a platform and language for server-side and other programming.

JavaScript, on the other hand, is a scripting language that was initially developed for use within web pages. The standardized version is ECMAScript. While its name is similar to Java, JavaScript was developed by Netscape and it has almost nothing to do with Java, although, like Java, its syntax is derived from the C programming language. In conjunction with a web page's Document Object Model, JavaScript has become a much more powerful technology than its creators originally envisioned. The manipulation of a page's Document Object Model after the page is delivered to the client has been called Dynamic HTML (DHTML), to emphasize a shift away from static HTML displays.

In its simplest form, all the optional information and actions available on a JavaScript-capable web page will have been downloaded when the page was first delivered. Ajax ("Asynchronous JavaScript And XML") is a JavaScript-based technology that may have a significant effect on the development of the World Wide Web. Ajax provides a method whereby large or small parts within a web page may be updated, using new information obtained over the network in response to user actions. This allows the page to be much more responsive, interactive and interesting, without the user having to wait for whole-page reloads. Ajax is seen as an important aspect of what is being called Web 2.0. Examples of Ajax techniques currently in use can be seen in Gmail, Google Maps, and other dynamic Web 2.0 web applications.

Web Pages

Web pages are available to individuals outside mass media. In order to publish a web page, one does not have to go through a publisher or other media institution, and potential readers could be found in all corners of the globe.

Unlike books and other documents, hypertext does not need to have a linear order from beginning to end. It is not necessarily broken down into the hierarchy of chapters, sections, subsections, and so on. Many different kinds of information are now available on the Web, and for those who wish to know other societies, cultures, and peoples, it has become easier. When traveling in a foreign country or a remote town, one might be able to find some information about the place on the Web, especially if the place is in one of the developed countries. Local newspapers, government publications, and other materials are easier to access, and therefore the variety of information obtainable with the same effort may be said to have increased for the users of the Internet.

Although some web sites are available in multiple languages, many are in the local language only. Additionally, not all software supports all special characters, and RTL languages. These factors would challenge the notion that the World Wide Web will bring a unity to the world.

The increased opportunity to publish materials is certainly observable in the countless personal pages, as well as pages by families, small shops, etc., facilitated by the emergence of free web hosting services.

According to a 2001 study, there were more than 550 billion documents on the Web, mostly in the "invisible web", or deep web. A 2002 survey of 2,024 million web pages determined that by far the most web content was in English: 56.4%; next were pages in German (7.7%), French (5.6%), and Japanese (4.9%). A more recent study, which used web searches in 75 different languages to sample the Web, determined that there were over 11.5 billion web pages in the publicly indexable web as of the end of January 2005.

Frustration over congestion issues in the Internet infrastructure and the high latency that results in slow browsing has led to an alternative, pejorative name for the World Wide Web: the World Wide Wait. Speeding up the Internet is an ongoing discussion over the use of peering and QoS technologies. Other solutions to reduce the World Wide Wait can be found on W3C.

2

History of World Wide Web

The Internet has revolutionized the computer and communications world like nothing before. The invention of the telegraph, telephone, radio, and computer set the stage for this unprecedented integration of capabilities. The Internet is at once a world-wide broadcasting capability, a mechanism for information dissemination, and a medium for collaboration and interaction between individuals and their computers without regard for geographic location.

The Internet represents one of the most successful examples of the benefits of sustained investment and commitment to research and development of information infrastructure. Beginning with the early research in packet switching, the government, industry and academia have been partners in evolving and deploying this exciting new technology.

The Internet today is a widespread information infrastructure, the initial prototype of what is often called the National Information Infrastructure. Its history is complex and involves many aspects - technological, organizational, and community. And its influence reaches not only to the technical fields of computer communications but throughout society as we move toward increasing use of online tools to accomplish electronic commerce, information acquisition, and community operations.

Origins of the Internet

The first recorded description of the social interactions that could be enabled through networking was a series of memos written by J.C.R. Licklider of MIT in August 1962 discussing his "Galactic Network" concept. He envisioned a globally interconnected set of computers through which everyone could quickly access data and programs from any site. In spirit, the concept was very much like the Internet of today. Licklider was the first head of the computer research program at DARPA, starting in October 1962. While at DARPA he convinced his successors at DARPA, Ivan Sutherland, Bob Taylor, and MIT researcher Lawrence G. Roberts, of the importance of this networking concept.

Leonard Kleinrock at MIT published the first paper on packet switching theory in July 1961 and the first book on the subject in 1964. Kleinrock convinced Roberts of the theoretical feasibility of communications using packets rather than circuits, which was a major step along the path towards computer networking. The other key step was to make the computers talk together. To explore this, in 1965 working with Thomas Merrill, Roberts connected the TX-2 computer in Mass. to the Q-32 in California with a low speed dial-up telephone line creating the first (however small) wide-area computer network ever built. The result of this experiment was the realization that the time-shared computers could work well together, running programs and retrieving data as necessary on the remote machine, but that the circuit switched telephone system was totally inadequate for the job. Kleinrock's conviction of the need for packet switching was confirmed.

In late 1966 Roberts went to DARPA to develop the computer network concept and quickly put together his plan for the "ARPANET", publishing it in 1967. At the conference where he presented the paper, there was also a paper on a packet network concept from the UK by Donald Davies and Roger Scantlebury of NPL. Scantlebury told Roberts about the NPL work as well as that of Paul Baran and others at RAND. The RAND group had written a paper on packet switching networks for secure voice in the military in 1964. It happened that the work at MIT (1961-1967), at RAND (1962-1965), and at NPL (1964-1967) had all proceeded in parallel without any of the researchers knowing about the other work. The word "packet" was adopted from the work at NPL and the proposed line speed to be used in the ARPANET design was upgraded from 2.4 kbps to 50 kbps.

In August 1968, after Roberts and the DARPA funded community had refined the overall structure and specifications for the ARPANET, an RFQ was released by DARPA for the development of one of the key components, the packet switches called Interface Message Processors (IMP's). The RFQ was won in December 1968 by a group headed by Frank Heart at Bolt Beranek and Newman (BBN). As the BBN team worked on the IMP's with Bob Kahn playing a major role in the overall ARPANET architectural design, the network topology and economics were designed and optimized by Roberts working with Howard Frank and his team at Network Analysis Corporation, and the network measurement system was prepared by Kleinrock's team at UCLA.

Due to Kleinrock's early development of packet switching theory and his focus on analysis, design and measurement, his Network Measurement Center at UCLA was selected to be the first node on the ARPANET. All this came together in September 1969 when BBN installed the first IMP at UCLA and the first host computer was connected. Doug Engelbart's project on "Augmentation of Human Intellect" (which included NLS, an early hypertext system) at Stanford Research Institute (SRI) provided a second node. SRI supported the Network Information Center, led by Elizabeth (Jake) Feinler and including functions such as maintaining tables of host name to address mapping as well as a directory of the RFC's. One month later, when SRI was connected to the ARPANET, the first host-to-host message was sent from Kleinrock's laboratory to SRI. Two more nodes were added at UC Santa Barbara and University of Utah. These last two nodes incorporated application visualization projects, with Glen Culler and Burton Fried at UCSB investigating methods for display of mathematical functions using storage displays to deal with the problem of refresh over the net, and Robert Taylor and Ivan Sutherland at Utah investigating methods of 3-D representations over the net. Thus, by the end of 1969, four host computers were connected together into the initial ARPANET, and the budding Internet was off the ground. Even at this early stage, it should be noted that the networking research incorporated both work on the underlying network and work on how to utilize the network. This tradition continues to this day.

Computers were added quickly to the ARPANET during the following years, and work proceeded on completing a functionally complete Host-to-Host protocol and other network software. In December 1970 the Network Working Group (NWG) working under S. Crocker finished the initial ARPANET Host-to-Host protocol, called the Network Control Protocol (NCP). As the ARPANET sites completed implementing NCP during the period 1971-1972, the network users finally could begin to develop applications.

In October 1972 Kahn organized a large, very successful demonstration of the ARPANET at the International Computer Communication Conference (ICCC). This was the first public demonstration of this new network technology to the public. It was also in 1972 that the initial "hot" application, electronic mail, was introduced. In March Ray Tomlinson at BBN wrote the basic email message send and read software, motivated by the need of the ARPANET developers for an easy coordination mechanism. In July, Roberts expanded its utility by writing the first email utility program to list, selectively read, file, forward, and respond to messages. From there email took off as the largest network application for over a decade. This was a harbinger of the kind of activity we see on the World Wide Web today, namely, the enormous growth of all kinds of "people-to-people" traffic.

Initial Internetting Concepts

The original ARPANET grew into the Internet. Internet was based on the idea that there would be multiple independent networks of rather arbitrary design, beginning with the ARPANET as the pioneering packet switching network, but soon to include packet satellite networks, ground-based packet radio networks and other networks. The Internet as we now know it embodies a key underlying technical idea, namely that of open architecture networking. In this approach, the choice of any individual network technology was not dictated by a particular network architecture but rather could be selected freely by a provider and made to interwork with the other networks through a meta-level "Internetworking Architecture". Up until that time there was only one general method for federating networks. This was the traditional circuit switching method where networks would interconnect at the circuit level, passing individual bits on a synchronous basis along a portion of an end-to-end circuit between a pair of end locations. Recall that Kleinrock had shown in 1961 that packet switching was a more efficient switching method. Along with packet switching, special purpose interconnection arrangements between networks were another possibility. While there were other limited ways to interconnect different networks, they required that one be used as a component of the other, rather than acting as a peer of the other in offering end-to-end service.

In an open-architecture network, the individual networks may be separately designed and developed and each may have its own unique interface which it may offer to users and/or other providers. including other Internet providers. Each network can be designed in accordance with the specific environment and user requirements of that network. There are generally no constraints on the types of network that can be included or on their geographic scope, although certain pragmatic considerations will dictate what makes sense to offer.

The idea of open-architecture networking was first introduced by Kahn shortly after having arrived at DARPA in 1972. This work was originally part of the packet radio program, but subsequently became a separate program in its own right. At the time, the program was called "Internetting". Key to making the packet radio system work was a reliable end-end protocol that could maintain effective communication in the face of jamming and other radio interference, or withstand intermittent blackout such as caused by being in a tunnel or blocked by the local terrain. Kahn first contemplated developing a protocol local only to the packet radio network, since that would avoid having to deal with the multitude of different operating systems, and continuing to use NCP.

However, NCP did not have the ability to address networks (and machines) further downstream than a destination IMP on the ARPANET and thus some change to NCP would also be required. (The assumption was that the ARPANET was not changeable in this regard). NCP relied on ARPANET to provide end-to-end reliability. If any packets were lost, the protocol (and presumably any applications it supported) would come to a grinding halt. In this model NCP had no end-end host error control, since the ARPANET was to be the only network in existence and it would be so reliable that no error control would be required on the part of the hosts.

Thus, Kahn decided to develop a new version of the protocol which could meet the needs of an open-architecture network environment. This protocol would eventually be called the Transmission Control Protocol/ Internet Protocol (TCP/IP). While NCP tended to act like a device driver, the new protocol would be more like a communications protocol.

Four ground rules were critical to Kahn's early thinking:

— Each distinct network would have to stand on its own and no internal changes could be required to any such network to connect it to the Internet.

— Communications would be on a best effort basis. If a packet didn't make it to the final destination, it would shortly be retransmitted from the source.

— Black boxes would be used to connect the networks; these would later be called gateways and routers. There would be no information retained by the gateways about the individual flows of packets passing through them, thereby keeping them simple and avoiding complicated adaptation and recovery from various failure modes.

— There would be no global control at the operations level.

Other key issues that needed to be addressed were:

— Algorithms to prevent lost packets from permanently disabling communications and enabling them to be successfully retransmitted from the source.

— Providing for host to host "pipelining" so that multiple packets could be enroute from source to destination at the discretion of the participating hosts, if the intermediate networks allowed it.

— Gateway functions to allow it to forward packets appropriately. This included interpreting IP headers for routing, handling interfaces, breaking packets into smaller pieces if necessary, etc.

— The need for end-end checksums, reassembly of packets from fragments and detection of duplicates, if any.

— The need for global addressing

— Techniques for host to host flow control.

— Interfacing with the various operating systems

— There were also other concerns, such as implementation efficiency, internetwork performance, but these were secondary considerations at first.

Kahn began work on a communications-oriented set of operating system principles while at BBN and documented some of his early thoughts in an internal BBN memorandum entitled "Communications Principles for Operating Systems". At this point he realized it would be necessary to learn the implementation details of each operating system to have a chance to embed any new protocols in an efficient way. Thus, in the spring of 1973, after starting the internetting effort, he asked Vint Cerf (then at Stanford) to work with him on the detailed design of the protocol. Cerf had been intimately involved in the original NCP design and development and already had the knowledge about interfacing to existing operating systems. So armed with Kahn's architectural approach to the communications side and with Cerf's NCP experience, they teamed up to spell out the details of what became TCP/IP.

The give and take was highly productive and the first written version 7 of the resulting approach was distributed at a special meeting of the International Network Working Group (INWG) which had been set up at a conference at Sussex University in September 1973. Cerf had been invited to chair this group and used the occasion to hold a meeting of INWG members who were heavily represented at the Sussex Conference.

Some basic approaches emerged from this collaboration between Kahn and Cerf:

— Communication between two processes would logically consist of a very long stream of bytes (they called them octets). The position of any octet in the stream would be used to identify it.

— Flow control would be done by using sliding windows and acknowledgments (acks). The destination could select when to acknowledge and each ack returned would be cumulative for all packets received to that point.

— It was left open as to exactly how the source and destination would agree on the parameters of the windowing to be used. Defaults were used initially.

— Although Ethernet was under development at Xerox PARC at that time, the proliferation of LANs were

> not envisioned at the time, much less PCs and workstations. The original model was national level networks like ARPANET of which only a relatively small number were expected to exist. Thus a 32 bit IP address was used of which the first 8 bits signified the network and the remaining 24 bits designated the host on that network. This assumption, that 256 networks would be sufficient for the foreseeable future, was clearly in need of reconsideration when LANs began to appear in the late 1970s.

The original Cerf/Kahn paper on the Internet described one protocol, called TCP, which provided all the transport and forwarding services in the Internet. Kahn had intended that the TCP protocol support a range of transport services, from the totally reliable sequenced delivery of data (virtual circuit model) to a datagram service in which the application made direct use of the underlying network service, which might imply occasional lost, corrupted or reordered packets.

However, the initial effort to implement TCP resulted in a version that only allowed for virtual circuits. This model worked fine for file transfer and remote login applications, but some of the early work on advanced network applications, in particular packet voice in the 1970s, made clear that in some cases packet losses should not be corrected by TCP, but should be left to the application to deal with. This led to a reorganization of the original TCP into two protocols, the simple IP which provided only for addressing and forwarding of individual packets, and the separate TCP, which was concerned with service features such as flow control and recovery from lost packets. For those applications that did not want the services of TCP, an alternative called the User Datagram Protocol (UDP) was added in order to provide direct access to the basic service of IP.

A major initial motivation for both the ARPANET and the Internet was resource sharing - for example allowing users on the packet radio networks to access the time sharing systems attached to the ARPANET. Connecting the two together was far more economical that duplicating these very expensive computers. However, while file transfer and remote login (Telnet) were very important applications, electronic mail has probably had the most significant impact of the innovations from that era. Email provided a new model of how people could communicate with each other, and changed the nature of collaboration, first in the building of the Internet itself and later for much of society.

There were other applications proposed in the early days of the Internet, including packet based voice communication (the precursor of Internet telephony), various models of file and disk sharing, and early "worm" programs that showed the concept of agents (and, of course, viruses). A key concept of the Internet is that it was not designed for just one application, but as a general infrastructure on which new applications could be conceived, as illustrated later by the emergence of the World Wide Web. It is the general purpose nature of the service provided by TCP and IP that makes this possible.

Proving the Ideas

DARPA let three contracts to Stanford (Cerf), BBN (Ray Tomlinson) and UCL (Peter Kirstein) to implement TCP/IP (it was simply called TCP in the Cerf/Kahn paper but contained both components). The Stanford team, led by Cerf, produced the detailed specification and within about a year there were three independent implementations of TCP that could interoperate. This was the beginning of long term experimentation and development to evolve and mature the Internet concepts and technology. Beginning with the first three networks (ARPANET, Packet Radio, and Packet Satellite) and their initial research communities, the experimental environment has grown to incorporate essentially every form of network and a very broad-based research and development community. With each expansion has come new challenges.

The early implementations of TCP were done for large time sharing systems such as Tenex and TOPS 20. When desktop computers first appeared, it was thought by some that TCP was too big and complex to run on a personal computer. David Clark and his research group at MIT set out to show that a compact and simple implementation of TCP was possible. They produced an implementation, first for the Xerox Alto (the early personal workstation developed at Xerox PARC) and then for the IBM PC. That implementation was fully interoperable with other TCPs, but was tailored to the application suite and performance objectives of the personal computer, and showed that workstations, as well as large time-sharing systems, could be a part of the Internet. In 1976, Kleinrock published the first book on the ARPANET. It included an emphasis on the complexity of protocols and the pitfalls they often introduce.

Widespread development of LANS, PCs and workstations in the 1980s allowed the nascent Internet to flourish. Ethernet technology, developed by Bob Metcalfe at Xerox PARC in 1973, is now probably the dominant network technology in the Internet and PCs and workstations the dominant computers. This change from having a few networks with a modest number of time-shared hosts (the original ARPANET model) to having many networks has resulted in a number of new concepts and changes to the underlying technology. First, it resulted in the definition of three network classes (A, B, and C) to accommodate the range of networks. Class A represented large national scale networks (small number of networks with large numbers of hosts); Class B represented regional scale networks; and Class C represented local area networks (large number of networks with relatively few hosts).

A major shift occurred as a result of the increase in scale of the Internet and its associated management issues. To make it easy for people to use the network, hosts were assigned names, so that it was not necessary to remember the numeric addresses. Originally, there were a fairly limited number of hosts, so it was feasible to maintain a single table of all the hosts and their associated names and addresses. The shift to having a large number of independently managed networks (e.g., LANs) meant that having a single table of hosts was no longer feasible, and the Domain Name System (DNS) was invented by Paul Mockapetris of USC/ISI. The DNS permitted a scalable distributed mechanism for resolving hierarchical host names into an Internet address.

The increase in the size of the Internet also challenged the capabilities of the routers. Originally, there was a single distributed algorithm for routing that was implemented uniformly by all the routers in the Internet. As the number of networks in the Internet exploded, this initial design could not expand as necessary, so it was replaced by a hierarchical model of routing, with an Interior Gateway Protocol (IGP) used inside each region of the Internet, and an Exterior Gateway Protocol (EGP) used to tie the regions together. This design permitted different regions to use a different IGP, so that different requirements for cost, rapid reconfiguration, robustness and scale could be accommodated. Not only the routing algorithm, but the size of the addressing tables, stressed the capacity of the routers. New approaches for address aggregation, in particular classless inter-domain routing (CIDR), have recently been introduced to control the size of router tables.

As the Internet evolved, one of the major challenges was how to propagate the changes to the software, particularly the host software. DARPA supported UC Berkeley to investigate modifications to the Unix operating system, including incorporating TCP/IP developed at BBN. Although Berkeley later rewrote the BBN code to more efficiently fit into the Unix system and kernel, the incorporation of TCP/IP into the Unix BSD system releases proved to be a critical element in dispersion of the protocols to the research community. Much of the CS research community began to use Unix BSD for their day-to-day computing environment. Looking back, the strategy of incorporating Internet protocols into a supported operating system for the research community was one of the key elements in the successful widespread adoption of the Internet.

One of the more interesting challenges was the transition of the ARPANET host protocol from NCP to TCP/IP as of January 1, 1983. This was a "flag-day" style transition, requiring all hosts to convert simultaneously or be left having to communicate via rather ad-hoc mechanisms. This transition was carefully planned within the community over several years before it actually took place and went surprisingly smoothly.

TCP/IP was adopted as a defense standard three years earlier in 1980. This enabled defense to begin sharing in the DARPA Internet technology base and led directly to the eventual partitioning of the military and non-military communities. By 1983, ARPANET was being used by a significant number of defense R&D and operational organizations. The transition of ARPANET from NCP to TCP/IP permitted it to be split into a MILNET supporting operational requirements and an ARPANET supporting research needs. Thus, by 1985, Internet was already well established as a technology supporting a broad community of researchers and developers, and was beginning to be used by other communities for daily computer communications. Electronic mail was being used broadly across several communities, often with different systems, but interconnection between different mail systems was demonstrating the utility of broad based electronic communications between people.

Transition to Widespread Infrastructure

At the same time that the Internet technology was being experimentally validated and widely used amongst a subset of computer science researchers, other networks and networking technologies were being pursued. The usefulness of computer networking - especially electronic mail - demonstrated by DARPA and Department of Defense contractors on the ARPANET was not lost on other communities and disciplines, so that by the mid-1970s computer networks had begun to spring up wherever funding could be found for the purpose.

The U.S. Department of Energy (DoE) established MFENet for its researchers in Magnetic Fusion Energy, whereupon DoE's High Energy Physicists responded by building HEPNet. NASA Space Physicists followed with SPAN, and Rick Adrion, David Farber, and Larry Landweber established CSNET for the (academic and industrial) Computer Science community with an initial grant from the U.S. National Science Foundation (NSF). AT&T's free-wheeling dissemination of the UNIX computer operating system spawned USENET, based on UNIX' built-in UUCP communication protocols, and in 1981 Ira Fuchs and Greydon Freeman devised BITNET, which linked academic mainframe computers in an "email as card images" paradigm.

With the exception of BITNET and USENET, these early networks (including ARPANET) were purpose-built - i.e., they were intended for, and largely restricted to, closed communities of scholars; there was hence little pressure for the individual networks to be compatible and, indeed, they largely were not. In addition, alternate technologies were being pursued in the commercial sector, including XNS from Xerox, DECNet, and IBM's SNA. 8 It remained for the British JANET (1984) and U.S. NSFNET (1985) programs to explicitly announce their intent to serve the entire higher education community, regardless of discipline. Indeed, a condition for a U.S. university to receive NSF funding for an Internet connection was that "... the connection must be made available to ALL qualified users on campus."

In 1985, Dennis Jennings came from Ireland to spend a year at NSF leading the NSFNET program. He worked with the community to help NSF make a critical decision - that TCP/IP would be mandatory for the NSFNET program. When Steve Wolff took over the NSFNET program in 1986, he recognized the need for a wide area networking infrastructure to support the general academic and research community, along with the need to develop a strategy for establishing such infrastructure on a basis ultimately independent of direct federal funding. Policies and strategies were adopted to achieve that end.

NSF also elected to support DARPA's existing Internet organizational infrastructure, hierarchically arranged under the (then) Internet Activities Board (IAB). The public declaration of this choice was the joint authorship by the IAB's Internet Engineering and Architecture Task Forces and by NSF's Network Technical

Advisory Group of RFC 985 (Requirements for Internet Gateways), which formally ensured interoperability of DARPA's and NSF's pieces of the Internet. In addition to the selection of TCP/IP for the NSFNET program, Federal agencies made and implemented several other policy decisions which shaped the Internet of today.

Federal agencies shared the cost of common infrastructure, such as trans-oceanic circuits. They also jointly supported "managed interconnection points" for interagency traffic; the Federal Internet Exchanges (FIX-E and FIX-W) built for this purpose served as models for the Network Access Points and "*IX" facilities that are prominent features of today's Internet architecture.

To coordinate this sharing, the Federal Networking Council 9 was formed. The FNC also cooperated with other international organizations, such as RARE in Europe, through the Coordinating Committee on Intercontinental Research Networking, CCIRN, to coordinate Internet support of the research community worldwide.

This sharing and cooperation between agencies on Internet-related issues had a long history. An unprecedented 1981 agreement between Farber, acting for CSNET and the NSF, and DARPA's Kahn, permitted CSNET traffic to share ARPANET infrastructure on a statistical and no-metered-settlements basis.

Subsequently, in a similar mode, the NSF encouraged its regional (initially academic) networks of the NSFNET to seek commercial, non-academic customers, expand their facilities to serve them, and exploit the resulting economies of scale to lower subscription costs for all.

On the NSFNET Backbone - the national-scale segment of the NSFNET - NSF enforced an "Acceptable Use Policy" (AUP) which prohibited Backbone usage for purposes "not in support of Research and Education." The predictable (and intended) result of encouraging commercial network traffic at the local and regional level, while denying its access to national-scale transport, was to stimulate the emergence and/or growth of "private", competitive, long-haul networks such as PSI, UUNET, ANS CO+RE, and (later) others. This process of privately-financed augmentation for commercial uses was thrashed out starting in 1988 in a series of NSF-initiated conferences at Harvard's Kennedy School of Government on "The Commercialization and Privatization of the Internet" - and on the "com-priv" list on the net itself.

In 1988, a National Research Council committee, chaired by Kleinrock and with Kahn and Clark as members, produced a report commissioned by NSF titled "Towards a National Research Network". This report was influential on then Senator Al Gore, and ushered in high speed networks that laid the networking foundation for the future information superhighway.

In 1994, a National Research Council report, again chaired by Kleinrock (and with Kahn and Clark as members again), Entitled "Realizing The Information Future: The Internet and Beyond" was released. This report, commissioned by NSF, was the document in which a blueprint for the evolution of the information superhighway was articulated and which has had a lasting affect on the way to think about its evolution. It anticipated the critical issues of intellectual property rights, ethics, pricing, education, architecture and regulation for the Internet.

NSF's privatization policy culminated in April, 1995, with the defunding of the NSFNET Backbone. The funds thereby recovered were (competitively) redistributed to regional networks to buy national-scale Internet connectivity from the now numerous, private, long-haul networks.

The backbone had made the transition from a network built from routers out of the research community (the "Fuzzball" routers from David Mills) to commercial equipment. In its 8 1/2 year lifetime, the Backbone had grown from six nodes with 56 kbps links to 21 nodes with multiple 45 Mbps links. It had seen the Internet grow to over 50,000 networks on all seven continents and outer space, with approximately 29,000 networks in the United States.

Such was the weight of the NSFNET program's ecumenism and funding ($200 million from 1986 to 1995) - and the quality of the protocols themselves - that by 1990 when the ARPANET itself was finally decommissioned10, TCP/IP had supplanted or marginalized most other wide-area computer network protocols worldwide, and IP was well on its way to becoming THE bearer service for the Global Information Infrastructure.

Role of Documentation

A key to the rapid growth of the Internet has been the free and open access to the basic documents, especially the specifications of the protocols. The beginnings of the ARPANET and the Internet in the university research community promoted the academic tradition of open publication of ideas and results. However, the normal cycle of traditional academic publication was too formal and too slow for the dynamic exchange of ideas essential to creating networks.

In 1969 a key step was taken by S. Crocker (then at UCLA) in establishing the Request for Comments (or RFC) series of notes. These memos were intended to be an informal fast distribution way to share ideas with other network researchers. At first the RFCs were printed on paper and distributed via snail mail. As the File Transfer Protocol (FTP) came into use, the RFCs were prepared as online files and accessed via FTP. Now, of course, the RFCs are easily accessed via the World Wide Web at dozens of sites around the world. SRI, in its role as Network Information Center, maintained the online directories. Jon Postel acted as RFC Editor as well as managing the centralized administration of required protocol number assignments, roles that he continued to play until his death, October 16, 1998.

The effect of the RFCs was to create a positive feedback loop, with ideas or proposals presented in one RFC triggering another RFC with additional ideas, and so on. When some consensus (or a least a consistent set of ideas) had come together a specification document would be prepared. Such a specification would then be used as the base for implementations by the various research teams.

Over time, the RFCs have become more focused on protocol standards (the "official" specifications), though there are still informational RFCs that describe alternate approaches, or provide background information on protocols and engineering issues. The RFCs are now viewed as the "documents of record" in the Internet engineering and standards community.

The open access to the RFCs (for free, if you have any kind of a connection to the Internet) promotes the growth of the Internet because it allows the actual specifications to be used for examples in college classes and by entrepreneurs developing new systems.

Email has been a significant factor in all areas of the Internet, and that is certainly true in the development of protocol specifications, technical standards, and Internet engineering. The very early RFCs often presented a set of ideas developed by the researchers at one location to the rest of the community. After email came into use, the authorship pattern changed - RFCs were presented by joint authors with common view independent of their locations.

The use of specialized email mailing lists has been long used in the development of protocol specifications, and continues to be an important tool. The IETF now has in excess of 75 working groups, each working on a different aspect of Internet engineering. Each of these working groups has a mailing list to discuss one or more draft documents under development. When consensus is reached on a draft document it may be distributed as an RFC.

As the current rapid expansion of the Internet is fueled by the realization of its capability to promote information sharing, we should understand that the network's first role in information sharing was sharing the information about it's own design and operation through the RFC documents. This unique method for evolving new capabilities in the network will continue to be critical to future evolution of the Internet.

Formation of the Broad Community

The Internet is as much a collection of communities as a collection of technologies, and its success is largely attributable to both satisfying basic community needs as well as utilizing the community in an effective way to push the infrastructure forward. This community spirit has a long history beginning with the early ARPANET.

The early ARPANET researchers worked as a close-knit community to accomplish the initial demonstrations of packet switching technology described earlier. Likewise, the Packet Satellite, Packet Radio and several other

DARPA computer science research programs were multi-contractor collaborative activities that heavily used whatever available mechanisms there were to coordinate their efforts, starting with electronic mail and adding file sharing, remote access, and eventually World Wide Web capabilities. Each of these programs formed a working group, starting with the ARPANET Network Working Group. Because of the unique role that ARPANET played as an infrastructure supporting the various research programs, as the Internet started to evolve, the Network Working Group evolved into Internet Working Group.

In the late 1970's, recognizing that the growth of the Internet was accompanied by a growth in the size of the interested research community and therefore an increased need for coordination mechanisms, Vint Cerf, then manager of the Internet Program at DARPA, formed several coordination bodies - an International Cooperation Board (ICB), chaired by Peter Kirstein of UCL, to coordinate activities with some cooperating European countries centered on Packet Satellite research, an Internet Research Group which was an inclusive group providing an environment for general exchange of information, and an Internet Configuration Control Board (ICCB), chaired by Clark. The ICCB was an invitational body to assist Cerf in managing the burgeoning Internet activity.

In 1983, when Barry Leiner took over management of the Internet research program at DARPA, he and Clark recognized that the continuing growth of the Internet community demanded a restructuring of the coordination mechanisms. The ICCB was disbanded and in its place a structure of Task Forces was formed, each focused on a particular area of the technology (e.g. routers, end-to-end protocols, etc.). The Internet Activities Board (IAB) was formed from the chairs of the Task Forces. It of course was only a coincidence that the chairs of the Task Forces were the same people as the members of the old ICCB, and Dave Clark continued to act as chair.

After some changing membership on the IAB, Phill Gross became chair of a revitalized Internet Engineering Task Force (IETF), at the time merely one of the IAB Task Forces. As we saw above, by 1985 there was a tremendous growth in the more practical/engineering side of the Internet. This growth resulted in an explosion in the attendance at the IETF meetings, and Gross was compelled to create substructure to the IETF in the form of working groups.

This growth was complemented by a major expansion in the community. No longer was DARPA the only major player in the funding of the Internet. In addition to NSFNet and the various US and international government-funded activities, interest in the commercial sector was beginning to grow. Also in 1985, both Kahn and Leiner left DARPA and there was a significant decrease in Internet activity at DARPA. As a result, the IAB was left without a primary sponsor and increasingly assumed the mantle of leadership.

The growth continued, resulting in even further substructure within both the IAB and IETF. The IETF combined Working Groups into Areas, and designated Area Directors. An Internet Engineering Steering Group (IESG) was formed of the Area Directors. The IAB recognized the increasing importance of the IETF, and restructured the standards process to explicitly recognize the IESG as the major review body for standards. The IAB also restructured so that the rest of the Task Forces (other than the IETF) were combined into an Internet Research Task Force (IRTF) chaired by Postel, with the old task forces renamed as research groups.

The growth in the commercial sector brought with it increased concern regarding the standards process itself. Starting in the early 1980's and continuing to this day, the Internet grew beyond its primarily research roots to include both a broad user community and increased commercial activity. Increased attention was paid to making the process open and fair. This coupled with a recognized need for community support of the Internet eventually led to the formation of the Internet Society in 1991, under the auspices of Kahn's Corporation for National Research Initiatives (CNRI) and the leadership of Cerf, then with CNRI.

In 1992, yet another reorganization took place. In 1992, the Internet Activities Board was re-organized and re-named the Internet Architecture Board operating under the auspices of the Internet Society. A more "peer" relationship was defined between the new IAB and IESG, with the IETF and IESG taking a larger responsibility for the approval of standards. Ultimately, a cooperative and mutually supportive relationship was formed between the IAB, IETF, and Internet Society, with the Internet Society taking on as a goal the provision of service and other measures which would facilitate the work of the IETF.

The recent development and widespread deployment of the World Wide Web has brought with it a new community, as many of the people working on the WWW have not thought of themselves as primarily network researchers and developers. A new coordination organization was formed, the World Wide Web Consortium (W3C). Initially led from MIT's Laboratory for Computer Science by Tim Berners-Lee (the inventor of the WWW) and Al Vezza, W3C has taken on the responsibility for evolving the various protocols and standards associated with the Web. Thus, through the over two decades of Internet activity, we have seen a steady evolution of organizational structures designed to support and facilitate an ever-increasing community working collaboratively on Internet issues.

Commercialization of the Technology

Commercialization of the Internet involved not only the development of competitive, private network services, but also the development of commercial products implementing the Internet technology. In the early 1980s, dozens of vendors were incorporating TCP/IP into their products because they saw buyers for that approach to networking. Unfortunately they lacked both real information about how the technology was supposed to work and how the customers planned on using this approach to networking. Many saw it as a nuisance add-on that had to be glued on to their own proprietary networking solutions: SNA, DECNet, Netware, NetBios. The DoD had mandated the use of TCP/IP in many of its purchases but gave little help to the vendors regarding how to build useful TCP/IP products.

In 1985, recognizing this lack of information availability and appropriate training, Dan Lynch in cooperation with the IAB arranged to hold a three day workshop for ALL vendors to come learn about how TCP/IP worked and what it still could not do well. The speakers came mostly from the DARPA research community who had both developed these protocols and used them in day to day work. About 250 vendor personnel came to listen to 50 inventors and experimenters. The results were surprises on both sides: the vendors were amazed to find that the inventors were so open about the way things worked and the inventors were pleased to listen to new problems they had not considered, but were being discovered by the vendors in the field. Thus a two way discussion was formed that has lasted for over a decade.

After two years of conferences, tutorials, design meetings and workshops, a special event was organized that invited those vendors whose products ran TCP/IP well enough to come together in one room for three days to show off how well they all worked together and also ran over the Internet. In September of 1988 the first Interop trade show was born. 50 companies made the cut. 5,000 engineers from potential customer organizations came to see if it all did work as was promised. It did. Why? Because the vendors worked extremely hard to ensure that everyone's products interoperated with all of the other products - even with those of their competitors. The Interop trade show has grown immensely since then and today it is held in 7 locations around the world each year to an audience of over 250,000 people who come to learn which products work with each other in a seamless manner, learn about the latest products, and discuss the latest technology.

In parallel with the commercialization efforts that were highlighted by the Interop activities, the vendors began to attend the IETF meetings that were held 3 or 4 times a year to discuss new ideas for extensions of the TCP/IP protocol suite. Starting with a few hundred attendees mostly from academia and paid for by the government, these meetings now often exceeds a thousand attendees, mostly from the vendor community and paid for by the attendees themselves. This self-selected group evolves the TCP/IP suite in a mutually cooperative manner. The reason it is so useful is that it is comprised of all stakeholders: researchers, end users and vendors.

Network• management provides an example of the interplay between the research and commercial communities. In the beginning of the Internet, the emphasis was on defining and implementing protocols that achieved interoperation. As the network grew larger, it became clear that the sometime ad hoc procedures used to manage the network would not scale. Manual configuration of tables was replaced by distributed automated algorithms, and better tools were devised to isolate faults. In 1987 it became clear that a protocol was needed that would permit the elements of the network, such as the routers, to be remotely managed in a uniform way. Several protocols for this purpose were proposed, including Simple Network Management Protocol or SNMP (designed, as its name would suggest, for simplicity, and derived from an earlier proposal called SGMP) , HEMS (a more complex design from the research community) and CMIP (from the OSI community). A series of meeting led to the decisions that HEMS would be withdrawn as a candidate for standardization, in order to help resolve the contention, but that work on both SNMP and CMIP would go forward, with the idea that the SNMP could be a more near-term solution and CMIP a longer-term approach. The market could choose the one it found more suitable. SNMP is now used almost universally for network based management.

In the last few years, we have seen a new phase of commercialization. Originally, commercial efforts mainly comprised vendors providing the basic networking products, and service providers offering the connectivity and basic Internet services. The Internet has now become almost a "commodity" service, and much of the latest attention has been on the use of this global information infrastructure for support of other commercial services. This has been tremendously accelerated by the widespread and rapid adoption of browsers and the World Wide Web technology, allowing users easy access to information linked throughout the globe. Products are available to facilitate the provisioning of that information and many of the latest developments in technology have been aimed at providing increasingly sophisticated information services on top of the basic Internet data communications.

Development of Web

The World Wide Web is a global information medium which users can read and write via computers connected to the Internet. The term is often mistakenly used as a synonym for the Internet itself, but the Web is a service that operates over the Internet, as e-mail does. The history of the Internet dates back significantly further than that of the World Wide Web. The hypertext portion of the Web has an interesting history, notable influences being IBM's Generalized Markup Language and Ted Nelson's Project Xanadu. Since its implementation in the 1990s as an academic system for sharing papers, the World Wide Web has evolved far beyond what its creators imagined.

In 1980, the Englishman Tim Berners-Lee, an independent contractor at CERN, built ENQUIRE, as a personal database of people and software models, but also as a way to play with hypertext; each new page of information in ENQUIRE had to be linked to an existing page.

Another major development occurred when Bob Kahn and Vint Cerf introduced Transmission Control Protocol (TCP) in 1977 for cross-network connections. Although it had used the older Network Control Protocol (NCP) since its establishment in 1969, ARPANET and its associated networks slowly began a transition to the new protocol during the 1970s. In 1978, Internet Protocol was added to TCP, responsible for the routing of messages. The TCP/IP combination was officially adopted by ARPANET and its partners in 1983, redefining the Internet as networks using the TCP/IP network. The standardisation of network protocols helped lay the foundations for the later growth of the World Wide Web.

In 1984 Berners-Lee returned to CERN, and considered its problems of information presentation: physicists from around the world needed to share data, with no common machines and no common presentation software. He wrote a proposal in March 1989 for "a large hypertext database with typed links", but it generated little interest. His boss, Mike Sendall, encouraged Berners-Lee to begin implementing his system on a newly acquired NeXT workstation. He considered several names, including Information Mesh, The Information Mine (turned down as it abbreviates to TIM, the WWW's creator's name) or Mine of Information (turned down because it abbreviates to MOI which is "Me" in French), but settled on World Wide Web.

By Christmas 1990, Berners-Lee had built all the tools necessary for a working Web: the first Web browser, WorldWideWeb (which was also a Web editor), the first Web server (info.cern.ch), and the first Web pages that described the project itself. The browser could access Usenet newsgroups and FTP files as well. However, it could run only on the NeXT; Nicola Pellow therefore created a simple text browser that could run on almost any computer. To encourage use within CERN, they put the CERN telephone directory on the web — previously users had had to log onto the mainframe in order to look up phone numbers.

Paul Kunz from the Stanford Linear Accelerator Center visited CERN in May 1991, and was captivated by the Web. He brought the NeXT software back to SLAC, where librarian Louise Addis adapted it for the VM/CMS operating system on the IBM mainframe as a way to display SLAC's catalog of online documents; this was the first web server outside CERN and the first in North America.

On August 6, 1991, Berners-Lee posted a short summary of the World Wide Web project on the alt.hypertext newsgroup. This date also marked the debut of the Web as a publicly available service on the Internet.

The WorldWideWeb (WWW) project aims to allow links to be made to any information anywhere. [...] The WWW project was started to allow high energy physicists to share data, news, and documentation. We are very interested in spreading the web to other areas, and having gateway servers for other data. Collaborators welcome!" —from Tim Berners-Lee's first message

Growth of the WWW

In keeping with its birth at CERN, early adopters of the World Wide Web were primarily university-based scientific departments or physics laboratories such as Fermilab and SLAC.

Early websites intermingled links for both the HTTP web protocol and the then-popular Gopher protocol, which provided access to content through hypertext menus presented as a file system rather than through HTML files. Early Web users would navigate either by bookmarking popular directory pages, such as Berners-Lee's first site at http://info.cern.ch/, or by consulting updated lists such as the NCSA "What's New" page. Some sites were also indexed by WAIS, enabling users to submit full-text searches similar to the capability later provided by search engines.

There was still no graphical browser available for computers besides the NeXT. This gap was filled in April 1992 with the release of Erwise, an application developed at Helsinki University of Technology, and in May by ViolaWWW, created by Pei-Yuan Wei, which included advanced features such as embedded graphics, scripting, and animation. Both programs ran on the X Window System for Unix.

Students at the University of Kansas adapted an existing text-only hypertext browser, Lynx, to access the web. Lynx was available on Unix and DOS, and some web designers, unimpressed with glossy graphical websites, held that a website not accessible through Lynx wasn't worth visiting.

Early Browsers

The turning point for the World Wide Web was the introduction of the Mosaic web browser in 1993, a graphical browser developed by a team at the National Center for Supercomputing Applications at the University of Illinois at Urbana-Champaign (NCSA-UIUC), led by Marc Andreessen. Funding for Mosaic came from the High-Performance Computing and Communications Initiative, a funding program initiated by then-Senator Al Gore's High Performance Computing and Communication Act of 1991 also known as the Gore Bill..

The origins of Mosaic begin in 1992. In November 1992, the National Center for Supercomputing Applications (NCSA) at the University of Illinois at Urbana-Champaign (UIUC) established a website. In December 1992, Andreessen and Eric Bina, students attending UIUC and working at the NCSA, began work on Mosaic. They released an X Window browser in February 1993. It gained popularity due to its strong support of integrated multimedia, and the authors' rapid response to user bug reports and recommendations for new features.

After graduation, Andreessen and Jim Clark, former CEO of Silicon Graphics, met and formed Mosaic Communications Corporation to develop the Mosaic browser commercially. The company changed its name to

Netscape in April 1994, and the browser was developed further as Netscape Navigator.

The first Microsoft Windows browser was Cello, written by Thomas R. Bruce for the Legal Information Institute at Cornell Law School to provide legal information, since most lawyers had access to Windows but not to Unix. Cello was released in June 1993.

In May 1994 the first International WWW Conference, organized by Robert Cailliau, was held at CERN; the conference has been held every year since. In April CERN had agreed that anyone could use the Web protocol and code royalty-free; this was in part a reaction to the perturbation caused by the University of Minnesota announcing that it would begin charging license fees for its implementation of the Gopher protocol.

In September 1994, the World Wide Web Consortium was founded at the Massachusetts Institute of Technology as an industry organization, with Tim Berners-Lee as director.

By 1996 it became obvious to most publicly traded companies that a public Web presence was no longer optional. Though at first people saw mainly the possibilities of free publishing and instant worldwide information, increasing familiarity with two-way communication over the "Web" led to the possibility of direct Web-based commerce (e-commerce) and instantaneous group communications worldwide. These concepts in turn intrigued many bright, young, often underemployed people (many of Generation X), who realized that new business models would soon arise based on these possibilities, and wanted to be among the first to profit from these new models.

An annual event started in 1995, the Webby Awards, working to recognize the best websites on the Internet.

The event was typically an extravaganza held annually in San Francisco, California, 45 miles north of the heart of Silicon Valley.

Given its early start, Netscape was the web browser of choice for approximately 80% of users in 1996. The release of Internet Explorer 4 in 1997 and the exploitation of its desktop operating system monopoly pushed Microsoft to about 90% market share by 2001 (when IE 6 was released). In 1998, Netscape released the source code of its flagship product as the open source browser Mozilla. It was soon decided that further development of the Netscape code base would be too complicated, and the browser was re-written from scratch. By 2006, Mozilla-based browsers including Firefox and other competition had reduced Internet Explorer's market share from its peak of about 95% down to around 85%.

The low interest rates in 1998–99 helped increase the start-up capital amounts. Although a number of these new entrepreneurs had realistic plans and administrative ability, most of them lacked these characteristics but were able to sell their ideas to investors because of the novelty of the dot-com concept.

Historically, the dot-com boom can be seen as similar to a number of other technology-inspired booms of the past including railroads in the 1840s, radio in the 1920s, transistor electronics in the 1950s, computer time-sharing in the 1960s, and home computers and biotechnology in the early 1980s. In 2001 the bubble burst, and many dot-com startups went out of business after burning through their venture capital and failing to become profitable.

Current Trends

The success of the Google search engine helped drive a resurgence in Internet advertising. In the aftermath of the dot-com bubble, the World Wide Web continued to gain popularity even though many businesses trying to exploit it went bankrupt. Also during this time, however, a handful of companies discovered success developing business models that would not exist if not for the World Wide Web. These include Google's search engine and its system of "relevant advertising", Apple Computer's iTunes web music store and Expedia's web-based travel service. Other companies, while offering traditional services, managed to find a solid Web-based niche and survive the bust; these include Amazon.com (books and media) and eBay (auctions). This era also brought social networking websites to light, that along with iTunes, are today an extensive part of youth culture, such as MySpace, and also Bebo, Xanga, Friendster, Facebook and orkut.

A New dot-com boom occurred starting in 2004 with first MySpace, and second, the permanent placement of Google in the popular culture spotlight, as well as the rapid popularization of Wikipedia and its sister projects, a website proven revolutionary for promoting the User edited content concept. In 2005, 3 ex-PayPal employees formed a video viewing website called YouTube. Only a year later, YouTube was proven the most quickly popularized website in history, and even started a new concept of user-submitted content in major events, as in the CNN-YouTube Presidential Debates.

The latest extension of the World Wide Web has focused on connecting devices to the Internet, coined Intelligent Device Management. As Internet connectivity becomes more easily accessible, manufacturers have started to leverage the expanded computing power of their devices to enhance their usability and capability. Through Internet connectivity, manufacturers are now able to interact with the devices they have sold and shipped to their customers, monitor device performance, provide enhanced customer support, and offer their customers new complimentary services, even after the products have been shipped to the customer location. A new breed of software companies, such as Questra Corporation, Esprida, Axeda, and NextNine have emerged to leverage the ubiquitous Internet to help manufacturers enhance the products they sell and develop innovative services for their customers.

The Internet has changed much in the two decades since it came into existence. It was conceived in the era of time-sharing, but has survived into the era of personal computers, client-server and peer-to-peer computing, and the network computer. It was designed before LANs existed, but has accommodated that new network technology, as well as the more recent ATM and frame switched services. It was envisioned as supporting a range of functions from file sharing and remote login to resource sharing and collaboration, and has spawned electronic mail and more recently the World Wide Web. But most important, it started as the creation of a small band of dedicated researchers, and has grown to be a commercial success with billions of dollars of annual investment.

One should not conclude that the Internet has now finished changing. The Internet, although a network in name and geography, is a creature of the computer, not the traditional network of the telephone or television industry. It will, indeed it must, continue to change and evolve at the speed of the computer industry if it is to remain relevant. It is now changing to provide such new services as real time transport, in order to support, for example, audio and video streams. The availability of pervasive networking (i.e., the Internet) along with powerful affordable computing and communications in portable form (i.e., laptop computers, two-way pagers, PDAs, cellular phones), is making possible a new paradigm of nomadic computing and communications.

This evolution will bring us new applications - Internet telephone and, slightly further out, Internet television. It is evolving to permit more sophisticated forms of pricing and cost recovery, a perhaps painful requirement in this commercial world. It is changing to accommodate yet another generation of underlying network technologies with different characteristics and requirements, from broadband residential access to satellites. New modes of access and new forms of service will spawn new applications, which in turn will drive further evolution of the net itself.

The most pressing question for the future of the Internet is not how the technology will change, but how the process of change and evolution itself will be managed. As this paper describes, the architecture of the Internet has always been driven by a core group of designers, but the form of that group has changed as the number of interested parties has grown. With the success of the Internet has come a proliferation of stakeholders - stakeholders now with an economic as well as an intellectual investment in the network. We now see, in the debates over control of the domain name space and the form of the next generation IP addresses, a struggle to find the next social structure that will guide the Internet in the future. The form of that structure will be harder to find, given the large number of concerned stake-holders. At the same time, the industry struggles to find the economic rationale for the large investment needed for the future growth, for example to upgrade residential access to a more suitable technology. If the Internet stumbles, it will not be because we lack for technology, vision, or motivation. It will be because we cannot set a direction and march collectively into the future.

3

Web Design and Development

Web design is a process of conceptualization, planning, modeling, and execution of electronic media delivery via Internet in the form of Markup language suitable for interpretation by Web browser and display as Graphical user interface (GUI).

The intent of web design is to create a web site — a collection of electronic files that reside on a web server/servers and present content and interactive features/interfaces to the end user in form of Web pages once requested. Such elements as text, bit-mapped images (GIFs, JPEGs, PNGs), forms can be placed on the page using HTML/XHTML/XML tags. Displaying more complex media (vector graphics, animations, videos, sounds) requires plug-ins such as Flash, QuickTime, Java run-time environment, etc. Plug-ins are also embedded into web page by using HTML/XHTML tags.

Improvements in browsers' compliance with W3C standards prompted a widespread acceptance and usage of XHTML/XML in conjunction with Cascading Style Sheets (CSS) to position and manipulate web page elements and objects. Latest standards and proposals aim at leading to browsers' ability to deliver a wide variety of media and accessibility options to the client possibly without employing plug-ins.

Typically web pages are classified as static or dynamic.

Static pages don't change content and layout with every request unless a human (web master/programmer) manually updates the page.

Dynamic pages adapt their content and/or appearance depending on end-user's input/interaction or changes in the computing environment (user, time, database modifications, etc.) Content can be changed on the client side (end-user's computer) by using client-side scripting languages (JavaScript, JScript, Actionscript, etc.) to alter DOM elements (DHTML). Dynamic content is often compiled on the server utilizing server-side scripting languages (Perl, PHP, ASP, JSP, ColdFusion, etc.). Both approaches are usually used in complex applications.

With growing specialization in the information technology field there is a strong tendency to draw a clear line between web design and web development.

History of Web design

Tim Berners-Lee, the inventor of the World Wide Web, published a website in August 1991. Berners-Lee was the first to combine Internet communication with hypertext (which had also been around for decades, but limited to browsing information stored on a single computer, such as interactive CD-ROM design).

Websites are written in a markup language called HTML, and early versions of HTML were very basic, only giving websites basic structure (headings and paragraphs), and the ability to link using hypertext. This was new and different to existing forms of communication - users could easily navigate to other pages by following hyperlinks from page to page.

As the Web and web design progressed, the markup language used to make it became more complex and flexible, giving the ability to add objects like images and tables to a page. Features like tables, which were originally intended to be used to display tabular information, were soon subverted for use as invisible layout devices. With the advent of Cascading Style Sheets (CSS), table-based layout is increasingly regarded as outdated. Database integration technologies such as server-side scripting and design standards like CSS further changed and enhanced the way the Web is made.

The introduction of Macromedia Flash (now Adobe Flash) into an already interactivity-ready scene has further changed the face of the Web, giving new power to designers and media creators, and offering new interactivity features to users, often at the expense of usability for persons with disabilities, search engine visibility and browser functions available to HTML.

Web Site Sesign

A Web site is a collection of information about a particular topic or subject. Designing a website is defined as the arrangement and creation of Web pages that in turn make up a website. A Web page consists of information for which the Web site is developed. A website might be compared to a book, where each page of the book is a web page.

There are many aspects (design concerns) in this process, and due to the rapid development of the Internet, new aspects may emerge. For typical commercial Web sites, the basic aspects of design are:

— *The content*: The substance, and information on the site should be relevant to the site and should target the area of the public that the website is concerned with.

— *The usability*: The site should be user-friendly, with the interface and navigation simple and reliable.

— *The appearance:* The graphics and text should include a single style that flows throughout, to show consistency. The style should be professional, appealing and relevant.

— *The visibility*: The site must also be easy to find via most, if not all, major search engines and advertisement media.

A Web site typically consists of text and images. The first page of a website is known as the Home page or Index. Some websites use what is commonly called a Splash Page. Splash pages might include a welcome message, language/ region selection, or disclaimer. Each web page within a Web site is an HTML file which has its own URL. After each Web page is created, they are typically linked together using a navigation menu composed of hyperlinks. Faster browsing speeds have led to shorter attention spans and more demanding online visitors and this has resulted in less use of Splash Pages, particularly where commercial websites are concerned.

Once a Web site is completed, it must be published or uploaded in order to be viewable to the public over the internet. This may be done using an FTP client. Once published, the Web master may use a variety of techniques to increase the traffic, or hits, that the website receives. This may include submitting the Web site to a search engine such as Google or Yahoo, exchanging links with other Web sites, creating affiliations with similar Web sites, etc.

Web site design crosses multiple disciplines of information systems, information technology and communication design. The website is an information system whose components are sometimes classified as front-end and back-end. The observable content (e.g page layout, user interface, graphics, text, audio) is known as the front-end. The back-end comprises the organization and efficiency of the source code, invisible scripted functions, and the server-side components that process the output from the front-end. Depending on the size of a Web development project, it may be carried out by a multi-skilled individual (sometimes called a web master), or a project manager may oversee collaborative design between group members with specialized skills.

Issues in Web Design

As in most collaborative designs, there are conflicts between differing goals and methods of web site designs. These are a few of the ongoing ones.

Lack of Collaboration in Design

In the early stages of the web, there wasn't as much collaboration between web designs and larger advertising campaigns, customer transactions, social networking, intranets and extranets as there is now. Web pages were mainly static online brochures disconnected from the larger projects. Many web pages are still disconnected from larger projects. Special design considerations are necessary for use within these larger projects. These design considerations are often overlooked, especially in cases where there is a lack of leadership, understanding or concern for the larger project to facilitate collaboration. This often results in unhealthy competition or compromise between departments, and less than optimal use of web pages.

Liquid versus Fixed Layouts

On the web the designer has no control over several factors, including the size of the browser window, the web browser used, the input devices used (mouse, touch screen, voice command, text, cell phone number pad, etc.) and the size and characteristics of available fonts.

Some designers choose to control the appearance of the elements on the screen by using specific width designations. This control may be achieved through the use of a HTML table-based design, or through the use of CSS. Whenever the text, images, and layout of a design do not change as the browser changes, this is referred to as a fixed width design. Proponents of fixed width design prefer the control over the look and feel of the site and the precision placement of objects on the page. Other designers choose a liquid design.

A liquid design is one, like Wikipedia, where the design moves to flow content into the whole screen, or a portion of the screen, no matter what the size of the browser window. Proponents of liquid design prefer to use all the screen space available. Liquid design can be achieved through the use of CSS, by avoiding styling the page altogether, or by using HTML tables set to a percentage of the page.

Both liquid and fixed design developers must make decisions about how the design should degrade on higher and lower screen resolutions. Sometimes the pragmatic choice is made to flow the design between a minimum and a maximum width. This allows the designer to avoid coding for the browser choices making up the long tail, while still using all available screen space.

Similar to liquid layout is the optional fit to window feature with Adobe Flash content. This is a fixed layout that optimally scales the content of the page without changing the arrangement or text wrapping when the browser is resized.

Flash

Adobe Flash (formerly Macromedia Flash) is a proprietary, robust graphics animation/application development program used to create and deliver dynamic content, media (such as sound and video), and interactive applications over the web via the browser.

Flash is not a standard produced by a vendor-neutral standards organization like most of the core protocols and formats on the Internet. Flash is much more restrictive than the open HTML format, though, requiring a proprietary plugin to be seen, and it does not integrate with most web browser UI features like the "Back" button unless a hyperlink is programmed to link a new html page from the Flash file, in which case the animation of the previous page would reset. However, those restrictions may be irrelevant depending on the goals of the web site design.

According to a study , 98% of US Web users have the Flash Player installed , with 45%-56% (depending on region) having the latest version. Numbers vary depending on the detection scheme and research demographics.

Many graphic artists use Flash because it gives them exact control over every part of the design, and anything can be animated and generally "jazzed up". Some application designers enjoy Flash because it lets them create applications that don't have to be refreshed or go to a new web page every time an action occurs. Flash can use embedded fonts instead of the standard fonts installed on most computers. There are many sites which forgo HTML entirely for Flash. Other sites may use Flash content combined with HTML as conservatively as gifs or jpegs would be used, but with smaller vector file sizes and the option of faster loading animations. Flash may also be used to protect content from unauthorized duplication or searching.

Flash detractors claim that Flash websites tend to be poorly designed, and often use confusing and non-standard user-interfaces. Up until recently, search engines have been unable to index Flash objects, which has prevented sites from having their contents easily found. This is because many search engine crawlers rely on text to index websites. It is possible to specify alternate content to be displayed for browsers that do not support Flash. Using alternate content also helps search engines to understand the page, and can result in much better visibility for the page. However, the vast majority of Flash websites are not disability accessible (for screen readers, for example) or Section 508 compliant. An additional issue is that sites which commonly use alternate content for search engines to their human visitors are usually judged to be spamming search engines and are automatically banned.

The most recent incarnation of Flash's scripting language (called "ActionScript", which is an ECMA language similar to JavaScript) incorporates long-awaited usability features, such as respecting the browser's font size and allowing blind users to use screen readers. Actionscript 2.0 is an Object-Oriented language, allowing the use of CSS, XML, and the design of class-based web applications.

Tableless Web Design

Tableless Web design (or tableless web layout) is a method of web design and development without using HTML tables for page layout control purposes. Instead of HTML tables, style sheet languages such as CSS (Cascading Style Sheets) are used to arrange elements and text on a web page. CSS was introduced by the World Wide Web Consortium (W3C) to improve web accessibility and to make HTML code semantic rather than presentational.

Early in its advent, many web developers considered CSS a more powerful and easier to use way of formatting, and considered the <FONT> tag obsolete. On the other hand early CSS had very limited and difficult to use layout capabilities and many common page layouts (like the 3-column design) that were very easy to implement with tables had no obvious equivalents in CSS.

As of 2006, CSS layout capabilities improved considerably. However, many popular browsers have limited or buggy support for these newer features of CSS, which has slowed the adoption of tableless web design. Many websites still use CSS for text formatting only, while using tables for layout.

HTML was originally designed as a semantic markup language intended for sharing scientific documents and research papers online. However, as the Internet expanded from the academic and research world into the mainstream in the mid 1990s, and became more media oriented, graphic designers sought for ways to control the visual appearance of the Web pages presented to end users. To this end, tables and spacers (usually transparent single pixel GIF images with explicitly specified width and height) have been used to create and maintain page layout.

This causes a number of problems. Many Web pages have been designed with tables nested within tables, resulting in large HTML documents which use more bandwidth than documents with simpler formatting. Furthermore, when a table based layout is linearized, for example when being parsed by a screen reader or a search engine, the resulting order of the content can be somewhat jumbled and confusing.

As a consequence of this trend, CSS was developed to improve the separation between design and content, and move back towards a semantic organization of content on the Web. In addition, a web browser usually has to download all content within a table before displaying it on a page, resulting in slower-seeming load times. Without tables, content on a page can load sequentially, appearing faster to the end user.

Advantages

Web accessibility. Because of the rapid growth of the Internet, disability discrimination legislation, and the increasing use of mobile phones and PDAs, it is necessary for Web content to be made accessible to users operating a wide variety of devices. Tableless Web design considerably improves Web accessibility in this respect. Screen readers and braille devices have fewer problems with tableless designs because they follow a logical structure.

As a result of the separation of design (CSS) and structure (HTML), it is also possible to provide different layouts for different devices, e.g. handhelds, mobile phones, etc. It is also possible to specify a different style sheet for print, e.g. to hide or modify the appearance of advertisements or navigation elements that are irrelevant and a nuisance in the printable version of the page. The W3C's Web Content Accessibility Guidelines' guideline no. 3 states "use markup and style sheets and do so properly."The guideline's checkpoint 3.3, a priority-2 checkpoint, says "use style sheets to control layout and presentation."

Bandwidth savings. In general, a tableless design results in smaller, more compact Web pages. Tableless designs do away with the need for embedded tables and spacer images and can significantly reduce download times, save bandwidth and reduce the latency of the site. The CSS file can also be cached by the browser, thereby providing further savings in bandwidth, particularly for dynamically generated content as the layout information does not need to be reloaded with every page visit. These issues are particularly important on busy and popular sites, and on content that will be viewed by users with slow Internet connections (e.g. on mobile devices.)

Maintainability. Maintaining a website may require frequent changes, both small and large, to the visual style of a website, depending on the purpose of the site. Under table-based layout, the layout is part of the HTML itself. As such, without the aid of template-based visual editors such as HTML editors, changing the positional layout of elements on a global scale may require a great deal of effort, depending on the amount of repetitive changes required. Even employing grep or similar global find & replace utilities cannot alleviate the problem entirely.

In tableless layout using CSS, virtually all of the layout information resides in one place: the CSS document. Because the layout information is centralized, these changes can be made quickly and globally by default. The HTML files themselves do not, usually, need to be adjusted when making layout changes. If they do, it is usually to add class-tags to specific markup elements or to change the grouping of various sections with respect to one another.

Also, because the layout information is stored externally to the HTML, it is quite easy to add new content in a tableless design, whether modifying an existing page or adding a new page. By contrast, without such a design, the layout for each page may require a more time-consuming manual changing of each instance or global find & replace utilities. Lastly, if the HTML source code is to be edited by hand, the code is more visually readable without the table layout tags and other styling information.

The main problem with tableless design is the wide differences that are to be found in browser support. There are considerable differences in implementing a CSS layout for multiple browsers due to bugs and mis-interpretation of the standards by different browser developers. These necessitate a large number of complex hacks and workarounds in the CSS files, and Web pages need to be tested much more carefully on a wider variety of devices than with table-based design, as some of these bugs can render the content illegible on some browsers.

In addition, CSS support in some older browsers such as Netscape 4 is very incomplete, which can cause major problems if these browsers also need to be targeted.

Conversion to tableless web design has been slow also because of table to layer/css conversion software. HTML editors such as Adobe Dreamweaver can convert tables to layers back and forth. Though this would ease the conversion a little, complications exist in the exactness of the conversion. The centering of tables centered them on the page, but the centering of layers together on different screen resolutions requires some tinkering.

Use of tables

Because of the term "tableless web design", some have interpreted this design strategy as an unconditional repudiation of all tables in web design. This has caused some to avoid tables even when tables are appropriate. Using divisions to simulate a table for the display of tabular data is as much a design flaw as using tables to simulate a division. Some sources clarify this distinction by using the more specific term "tableless web layout".

Additionally, one distinction is sometimes missed: using tables in web design does not necessarily equate to using the table element (and related elements) defined in

HTML 4.0. Although the table element is by far the most common means of specifying tables in web design (both for "layout" and "tabular data") CSS also specifies a "table model" which allows the semantics of "tabular representation" to be applied using other elements as well. One reason this distinction is sometimes overlooked is because of spotty support for the CSS table model in web browsers.

Accessible Web design

Accessible Web design is the art of creating webpages that are accessible to everyone, using any device. It is especially important so that people with disabilities - whether due to accident, disease or old age - can access the information in Web pages and be able to navigate through the website.

To be accessible, web pages and sites must conform to certain accessibility principles. These can be grouped into the following main areas:

- use semantic markup that provides a meaningful structure to the document (i.e. web page)
- Semantic markup also refers to semantically organizing the web page structure and publishing web services description accordingly so that they can be recognized by other web services on different web pages. Standards for semantic web are set by IEEE
- use a valid markup language that conforms to a published DTD or Schema
- provide text equivalents for any non-text components (e.g. images, multimedia)
- use hyperlinks that make sense when read out of context.

— don't use frames

— use CSS rather than HTML Tables for layout.

— author the page so that when the source code is read line-by-line by user agents (such as a screen readers) it remains intelligible.

However, W3C permits an exception where tables for layout either make sense when linearized or an alternate version (perhaps linearized) is made available.

Website Planning

Before creating and uploading a website, it is important to take the time to plan exactly what is needed in the website. Thoroughly considering the audience or target market, as well as defining the purpose and deciding what content will be developed are extremely important.

Purpose

It is essential to define the purpose of the website as one of the first steps in the planning process. A purpose statement should show focus based on what the website will accomplish and what the users will get from it. A clearly defined purpose will help the rest of the planning process as the audience is identified and the content of the site is developed. Setting short and long term goals for the website will help make the purpose clear and plan for the future when expansion, modification, and improvement will take place. Also, goal-setting practices and measurable objectives should be identified to track the progress of the site and determine success.

Audience

Defining the audience is a key step in the website planning process. The audience is the group of people who are expected to visit your website – the market being targeted. These people will be viewing the website for a specific reason and it is important to know exactly what they are looking for when they visit the site. A clearly defined purpose or goal of the site as well as an understanding of what visitors want to do/feel when they come to your site will help to identify the target audience. Upon considering who is most likely to need/use the content, a list of characteristics common to the users such as:

— Audience characteristics

— Information preferences

— Computer specifications

— Web experience

Taking into account the characteristics of the audience will allow an effective website to be created that will deliver the desired content to the target audience.

Content

Content evaluation and organization requires that the purpose of the website be clearly defined. Collecting a list of the necessary content then organizing it according to the audience's needs is a key step in website planning. In the process of gathering the content being offered, any items that do not support the defined purpose or accomplish target audience objectives should be removed. It is a good idea to test the content and purpose on a focus group and compare the offerings to the audience needs. The next step is to organize the basic information structure by categorizing the content and organizing it according to user needs. Each category should be named with a concise and descriptive title that will become a link on the website. Planning for the site's content ensures that the wants/needs of the target audience and the purpose of the site will be fulfilled.

Compatibility and Restrictions

Because of the market share of modern browsers (depending on your target market), the compatibility of your website with the viewers is restricted. For instance, a website that is designed for the majority of websurfers will be limited to the use of valid XHTML 1.0 Strict or older, Cascading Style Sheets Level 1, and 1024x768 display resolution. This is because Internet Explorer is not fully W3C standards compliant with the modularity of XHTML 1.1 and the majority of CSS beyond 1. A target market of more alternative browser (e.g. Firefox and Opera) users allow for more W3C compliance and thus a greater range of options for a web designer.

Another restriction on webpage design is the use of different Image file formats. The majority of users can support GIF, JPEG, and PNG (with restrictions). Again Internet Explorer is the major restriction here, not fully supporting PNG's advanced transparency features, resulting in the GIF format still being the most widely used graphic file format for transparent images.

Many website incompatibilities go unnoticed by the designer and unreported by the users. The only way to be certain a website will work on a particular platform is to test it on that platform.

Planning documentation

Documentation is used to visually plan the site while taking into account the purpose, audience and content, to design the site structure, content and interactions that are most suitable for the website. Documentation may be considered a prototype for the website – a model which allows the website layout to be reviewed, resulting in suggested changes, improvements and/or enhancements. This review process increases the likelihood of success of the website.

First, the content is categorized and the information structure is formulated. The information structure is used to develop a document or visual diagram called a site map. This creates a visual of how the web pages will be interconnected, which helps in deciding what content will be placed on what pages. There are three main ways of diagramming the website structure:

— *Linear Website Diagrams* will allow the users to move in a predetermined sequence;

— *Hierarchical structures* provide more than one path for users to take to their destination;

— *Branch Design Website Diagrams* allow for many interconnections between web pages such as hyperlinks within sentences.

In addition to planning the structure, the layout and interface of individual pages may be planned using a storyboard. In the process of storyboarding, a record is made of the description, purpose and title of each page in the site, and they are linked together according to the most effective and logical diagram type. Depending on the number of pages required for the website, documentation methods may include using pieces of paper and drawing lines to connect them, or creating the storyboard using computer software. Some or all of the individual pages may be designed in greater detail as a website wireframe, a mock up model or comprehensive layout of what the page will actually look like. This is often done in a graphic program, or layout design program. The wireframe has no working functionality, only planning.

Web Development

Web development is a broad term for any activities related to developing a web site for the World Wide Web or an intranet. This can include e-commerce business development, web design, web content development, client-side/server-side coding, and web server configuration. However, among web professionals, "web development" usually refers only to the non-design aspects of building web sites, e.g. writing markup and coding. Web development can range from developing the simplest static single page of plain text to the most complex web-based internet applications, electronic businesses, or social network services.

For larger businesses and organizations, web development teams can consist of hundreds of people. Smaller organizations may only require a single permanent or contracting webmaster, or secondary assignment to related job positions such as a graphic designer and/or Information systems technician. Web development may be a collaborative effort between departments rather than the domain of a designated department.

Since the mid-1990s, web development has been one of the fastest growing industries in the world. In 1995 there were fewer than 10,000 web development companies in the United States alone and in 2005 there are over 30,000 such companies. The web development industry is expected to grow over 20% by 2010. The growth of this industry is being pushed by large businesses wishing to sell products and services to their customers and to automate business workflow, as well as the growth of many small web design and development companies.

In addition, cost of Web site development and hosting has dropped dramatically during this time. Instead of costing tens of thousands of dollars, as was the case for early websites, one can now develop a simple web site for less than a thousand dollars, depending on the complexity and amount of content. Smaller Web site development companies are now able to make web design accessible to both smaller companies and individuals further fueling the growth of the web development industry. As far as web development tools and platforms are concerned, there are many systems available to the public free of charge to aid in development. A popular example is the LAMP (Linux, Apache, MySQL, PHP), which is usually distributed free of charge. This fact alone has manifested into many people around the globe setting up new Web sites daily and thus contributing to increase in web development popularity. Another contributing factor has been the rise of easy to use WYSIWYG web development software, most prominently Microsoft FrontPage or Adobe Dreamweaver. Using such software, virtually anyone can develop a Web page in a matter of minutes. Knowledge of HyperText Markup Language (HTML), or other programming languages is not required, but recommended for professional results.

The next generation of web development tools uses the strong growth in LAMP and Microsoft .NET technologies to provide the Web as a way to run applications online. Web developers now help to deliver applications as Web services which were traditionally only available as applications on a desk based computer.

Instead of running executable code on a local computer, users are interacting with online applications to create new content. This has created new methods in communication and allowed for many opportunities to decentralize information and media distribution. Users are now able to interact with applications from many locations, instead of being tied to a specific workstation for their application environment. Examples of dramatic transformation in communication and commerce led by web development include e-commerce. Online auction sites such as eBay have changed the way consumers consume and purchase goods and services. Online resellers such as Amazon.com and Buy.com (among many, many others) have transformed the shopping and bargain hunting experience for many consumers. Another good example of transformative communication led by web development is the blog. Web applications such as WordPress and b2evolution have created easily implemented blog environments for individual Web sites. Open source content systems such as Typo3, Xoops, Joomla, and Drupal have extended web development into new modes of interaction and communication.

Typical Areas

Web Development can be split into many areas and a typical and basic web development hierarchy might consist of;

- Client Side Coding
  - CSS
  - XHTML (in accordance to modern web design standards, XHTML's use is replacing the older HTML)
  - Javascript
  - Flash (Adobe Flash Player is a ubiquitous client-side platform ready for RIAs. Flex 2 is also deployed to the Flash Player (version 9+))
- Server Side Coding
  - PHP and MySQL
  - ASP and MSSQL
  - ASP.NET and MSSQL
  - CGI and/or Perl

  - — Java, e.g. J2EE or WebObjects
  - — Python, e.g. Django (web framework)
  - — Ruby, e.g. Ruby on Rails
  - — ColdFusion
- — In practice, many web developers will also have interdisciplinary skills / roles, including:
  - — Graphic design / web design
  - — Information architecture and copywriting/ copyediting with web usability, accessibility and search engine optimisation in mind
  - — Project management, QA and other aspects common to IT development in general

The above list is a simple website development hierarchy and can be extended to include all client side and server side aspects. It is still important to remember that web development is generally split up into client side coding covering aspects such as the layout and design, then server side coding, which covers the website's functionality and back end systems.

Looking at these items from an "umbrella approach", client side coding such as XHTML is executed and stored on a local client (in a web browser) whereas server side code is not available to a client and is executed on a web server which generates the appropriate XHTML which is then sent to the client. As the nature of client side coding allows you to alter the HTML on a local client and refresh the pages with updated content (locally), web designers must bear in mind the importance and relavence to security with their server side scripts. If a server side script accepts content from a locally modified client side script, the web development of that page shows poor sanitization with relation to security.

Security Issues

Web development takes into account a lot of things, such as data entry error checking through forms, as well as sanitization of the data that is entered in those fields. Malicious practices such as SQL injection can be executed through users with ill intent yet only primitive knowledge of web development as a whole. Not only this, but scripts can be exploited to grant unauthorized access to the hacker to gain information such as email addresses, passwords and protected content.

Some of this is dependent on the server environment (most commonly Apache or Microsoft IIS) on which the scripting language, such as PHP, Ruby or ASP is running, and therefore is not necessarily down to the web developer themselves to maintain. However, stringent testing of web applications before public release is encouraged to prevent such exploits from occurring.

4

Web Application

A Web application or webapp is an application that is accessed via web over a network such as the Internet or an intranet. Web applications are popular due to the ubiquity of a client, sometimes called a thin client. The ability to update and maintain Web applications without distributing and installing software on potentially thousands of client computers is a key reason for their popularity. Web applications are used to implement Webmail, online retail sales, online auctions, wikis, discussion boards, Weblogs, MMORPGs and many other functions.

In earlier types of client-server computing, each application had its own client program which served as its user interface and had to be separately installed on each user's personal computer. An upgrade to the server part of the application would typically require an upgrade to the clients installed on each user workstation, adding to the support cost and decreasing productivity.

In contrast, Web applications dynamically generate a series of Web documents in a standard format supported by common browsers such as HTML/XHTML. Client-side scripting in a standard language such as JavaScript is commonly included to add dynamic elements to the user interface. Generally, each individual Web page is delivered to the client as a static document, but the sequence of pages can provide an interactive experience, as user input is returned through Web form elements embedded in the page markup. During the session, the Web browser interprets and displays the pages, and acts as the universal client for any Web application.

Interface

The Web interface places very few limits on client functionality. Through Java, JavaScript, DHTML, Flash and other technologies, application-specific methods such as drawing on the screen, playing audio, and access to the keyboard and mouse are all possible. Many services have worked to combine all of these into a more familiar interface that adopts the appearance of an operating system. General purpose techniques such as drag and drop are also supported by these technologies. Web developers often use client-side scripting to add functionality, especially to create an interactive experience that does not require page reloading (which many users find disruptive). Recently, technologies have been developed to coordinate client-side scripting with server-side technologies such as PHP. Ajax, a web development technique using a combination of various technologies, is an example of technology which creates a more interactive experience.

Technical Considerations

A significant advantage of building Web applications to support standard browser features is that they should perform as specified regardless of the operating system or OS version installed on a given client. Rather than creating clients for MS Windows, Mac OS X, GNU/Linux, and other operating systems, the application can be written once and deployed almost anywhere. However, inconsistent implementations of the HTML, CSS, DOM and other browser specifications can cause problems in web application development and support. Additionally, the ability of users to customize many of the display settings of their browser (such as selecting different font sizes, colors, and typefaces, or disabling scripting support) can interfere with consistent implementation of a Web application.

Another (less common) approach is to use Adobe Flash or Java applets to provide some or all of the user interface. Since most Web browsers include support for these technologies (usually through plug-ins), Flash- or Java-based applications can be implemented with much of the same ease of deployment. Because they allow the programmer greater control over the interface, they bypass many browser-configuration issues, although incompatibilities between Java or Flash implementations on the client can introduce different complications. Because of their architectural similarities to traditional client-server applications, with a somewhat "thick" client, there is some dispute over whether to call systems of this sort "Web applications"; an alternative term is "Rich Internet Application".

Structure

Though many variations are possible, a Web application is commonly structured as a three-tiered application. In its most common form, a Web browser is the first tier, an engine using some dynamic Web content technology (such as ASP, ASP.NET, CGI, ColdFusion, JSP/Java, PHP, Python, or Ruby On Rails) is the middle tier, and a database is the third tier. The Web browser sends requests to the middle tier, which services them by making queries and updates against the database and generates a user interface.

Business Use

An emerging strategy for application software companies is to provide Web access to software previously distributed as local applications. Depending on the type of application, it may require the development of an entirely different browser-based interface, or merely adapting an existing application to use different presentation technology. These programs allow the user to pay a monthly or yearly fee for use of a software application without having to install it on a local hard drive. A company which follows this strategy is known as an application service provider (ASP), and ASPs are currently receiving much attention in the software industry.

Writing Web Applications

There are many Web application frameworks which facilitate rapid application development by allowing the programmer to define a high-level description of the program. In addition, there is potential for the development of applications on Internet Operating Systems, although currently there are not many viable platforms that fit this model.

The use of Web application frameworks can often reduce the number of errors in a program, both by making the code more simple, and by allowing one team to concentrate just on the framework. In applications which are exposed to constant hacking attempts on the Internet, security-related problems caused by errors in the program are a big issue. Frameworks may also promote the use of best practices such as GET after POST.

The Web Application Security Consortium (WASC), CGI Security, and OWASP are projects developed with the intention of documenting how to avoid security problems in Web applications.

Web Application Framework

A web application framework is a software framework that is designed to support the development of dynamic websites, Web applications and Web services. The framework aims to alleviate the overhead associated with common activities used in Web development. For example, many frameworks provide libraries for database access, templating frameworks and session management, and often promote code reuse.

Common Gateway Interface

As the design of the World Wide Web was not inherently dynamic, early hypertext consisted of hand-coded HTML that was published on web servers. Any modifications to published pages needed to be performed by the pages' author. To provide a dynamic web page that reflected user inputs, the Common Gateway Interface (CGI) standard was introduced for interfacing external applications with web servers. CGI could adversely affect server load, though, since each request had to start a separate process..

Tighter Integration

Programmers wanted tighter integration with the web server to enable high traffic web applications. The Apache HTTP Server, for example, supports modules that can extend the web server with arbitrary code executions (such as mod_python) or forward specific requests to a web server that can handle dynamic content. Some web servers (such as Apache Tomcat) were specifically designed to handle dynamic content by executing code written in some languages, such as Java.

Web Languages

Around the same time, new languages were being developed specifically for use in the web, such as PHP and Active Server Pages.

Web Libraries

While the vast majority of languages available to programmers to use in creating dynamic web pages have libraries to help with common tasks, web applications often require specific libraries that are useful in web applications, such as creating HTML (for example, JavaServer Faces).

Full Stack

Eventually, mature, "full stack" frameworks appeared, that often gathered multiple libraries useful for web development into a single cohesive software stack for web developers to use. Examples of this include JavaEE, OpenACS and Ruby on Rails.

Architectures

Model View Controller

Many frameworks follow the Model View Controller (MVC) architectural pattern to separate the data model, business rules and user interface.

Push-based vs. Pull-based

Most MVC frameworks follow a push-based architecture. These frameworks use actions that do the required processing, and then "push" the data to the view layer to render the results. Struts and Ruby on Rails are good examples of this architecture.

An alternative to this is pull-based architecture, sometimes also called "component-based". These frameworks start with the view layer, which can then "pull" results from multiple controllers as needed. In this architecture, multiple controllers can be involved with a single view. Tapestry and JBoss Seam are examples of pull-based architectures.

FEATURES

Security

Some web application frameworks come with authentication and authorization frameworks, that enable the web server to identify the users of the application, and restrict access to functions based on some defined criteria. Django is one example that provides role-based access to pages, and provides a web-based interface for creating users and assigning them roles.

Database Access and Mapping

Many web application frameworks create a unified API to a database backend, enabling web applications to work with a variety of databases with no code changes, and allowing programmers to work with higher-level concepts. For higher performance, database connections should be pooled as e.g. AOLserver does. Additionally, some object-oriented frameworks contain mapping tools to provide Object-Relational Mapping, which will map objects to tuples.

Other features web application frameworks may provide include transactional support and database migration tools.

URL Mapping

By automatically rewriting a url with parameters to a friendly URL, the system becomes easier to use, and as an additional benefit, is better indexed by search engines.

Web Template System

Dynamic web pages usually consist of a static part (HTML) and a dynamic part, which is code that generates HTML. The code that generates the HTML can do this based on variables in a template, or on code. The text to be generated can come from a database, thereby making it possible to dramatically reduce the number of pages in a site.

Consider the example of a real estate agent with 500 houses for sale. In a static web site, the agent would have to create 500 pages in order to make the information available. In a dynamic website, the agent would simply connect the dynamic page to a database table of 500 records.

In a template, variables from the programming language can be inserted without using code, thereby losing the requirement of programming knowledge to make updates to the pages in a web site. A syntax is made available to distinguish between HTML and variables.

Many template engines do support limited logic tags, like IF and FOREACH. These are to be used only for decisions that need to be made for the presentation layer, in order to keep a clean separation from the business logic layer, or the M(odel) in the MVC pattern.

Some frameworks will generate a basic, but fully-functional, application, once the developer specifies the structure of the data, or it is discovered through introspection. In some frameworks, this scaffolding supports the create, read, update and delete (CRUD) operations necessary to manipulate data.

WEB CACHE

Web caching is the caching of web documents in order to reduce bandwidth usage, server load, and perceived "lag". A web cache stores copies of documents passing through it; subsequent requests may be satisfied from the cache if certain conditions are met. Some application frameworks provide mechanisms for caching documents and bypassing the web template system.

Ajax

Ajax, shorthand for "Asynchronous JavaScript and XML", is a web development technique for creating interactive web applications. The intent is to make web pages feel more responsive by exchanging small amounts of data with the server behind the scenes, so that the entire web page does not have to be reloaded each time the user requests a change. This is intended to increase the web page's interactivity, speed, and usability.

Due to complexity of Ajax programming, there are numerous Ajax frameworks that exclusively deal with Ajax support. Some Ajax frameworks are even embedded as a part of larger frameworks. For example, the Prototype JavaScript Framework is included in Ruby on Rails.

Automatic Configuration

Some frameworks minimize web application configuration through the use of introspection and/or following known conventions. For example, many Java frameworks use Hibernate as a persistence layer, which can generate a database schema at runtime capable of persisting the necessary information. This allows the application designer to design business objects without needing to explicitly define a database schema. Frameworks such as Ruby on Rails can also work in reverse, that is, define properties of model objects at runtime based on a database schema.

Technologies

Languages

Many languages have an associated web application framework. However, certain languages either have a critical mass of developers to give a higher level of support to frameworks, or provide features that prove conducive to the development of web application frameworks

Java

There are numerous Java frameworks either in development or in use. Many of these frameworks are built on top of, or borrow elements from the Java EE platform.

C# and VB.net

C# and VB.net are the most popular languages on the language neutral Microsoft's ASP.NET platform. One of the most popular web application frameworks of the early days is the DotNetNuke web application framework. Since ASP.NET itself is a technology designed for building web apps it's often wrongly referred to as only a web application framework. But this is definetely a very reduced view of ASP.net, besides all essential web application framework features you get independent of a certain programming language, you can choose your favourite language of .NET_Languages, but you are also strictly bound to the Microsoft Windows platform. Besides ordinary features ASP.net has also a Ajax framework integrated - ASP.NET AJAX .

PHP

PHP's original design for dynamic web pages has given support to projects such as CakePHP, PRADO, Qcodo, symfony, Zoop Framework, the eZ publish web publishing framework and the Zend Framework.

Perl, Python and Ruby

There are numerous dynamic language frameworks. Perl has Maypole, Catalyst, and Jifty. Python has Django, TurboGears, pylons, Quixote, and Karrigell. Ruby has Nitro and Ruby on Rails.

TCL

OpenACS is an open source web application framework designed for developing high traffic web applications in Tcl.

Smalltalk

Seaside is an open source web application framework for developing web applications in Smalltalk. Although the main development of Seaside happens in Squeak there exist ports for other Smalltalk dialects.

JavaScript

Helma is an open source web application framework / publishing system written in Java which uses Javascript as programming language.

Operating Systems

With very few exceptions, web application frameworks are based upon platform independent languages that run on a variety of platforms. While some frameworks may recommend particular configurations, most can run on Windows, Linux, Mac and other Unix-based platforms. A notable exception is DotNetNuke, written for the .NET Framework, that does not support the Mono runtime.

Rich Internet application

Rich Internet applications (RIA) are Web applications that have the features and functionality of traditional desktop applications. RIAs typically transfer the processing necessary for the user interface to the Web client but keep the bulk of the data (i.e., maintaining the state of the program, the data etc) back on the application server.

RIAs typically:

— run in a Web browser, or do not require software installation

— run locally in a secure environment called a sandbox

The term "Rich Internet Application" was introduced in a Macromedia white paper in March 2002, though the concept had been around for a number of years before that under different names such as:

— Remote Scripting, by Microsoft, circa 1998

— X Internet, by Forrester Research in October 2000

— Rich (Web) clients

— Rich web application

Traditional web applications centered all activity around a client-server architecture with a thin client. Under this system all processing is done on the server, and the client is only used to display static (in this case HTML) content. The biggest drawback with this system is that all interaction with the application must pass through the server, which requires data to be sent to the server, the server to respond, and the page to be reloaded on the client with the response. By using a client side technology which can execute instructions on the client's computer, RIAs can circumvent this slow and synchronous loop for many user interactions. This difference is somewhat analogous to the difference between "terminal and mainframe" and Client-server/Fat client approaches.

Internet standards have evolved slowly and continually over time to accommodate these techniques, so it is hard to draw a strict line between what constitutes an RIA and what does not. But all RIAs share one characteristic: they introduce an intermediate layer of code, often called a client engine, between the user and the server. This client engine is usually downloaded at the beginning of the application, and may be supplemented by further code downloads as the application progresses. The client engine acts as an extension of the browser, and usually takes over responsibility for rendering the application's user interface and for server communication.

What can be done in an RIA may be limited by the capabilities of the system used on the client. But in general, the client engine is programmed to perform application functions that its designer believes will enhance some aspect of the user interface, or improve its responsiveness when handling certain user interactions, compared to a standard Web browser implementation. Also, while simply adding a client engine does not force an application to depart from the normal synchronous pattern of interactions between browser and server, in most RIAs the client engine performs additional asynchronous communications with servers.

Benefits

Because RIAs employ a client engine to interact with the user, they are:

— *Richer*. They can offer user-interface behaviors not obtainable using only the HTML widgets available to standard browser-based Web applications. This richer functionality may include anything that can be implemented in the technology being used on the client side, including drag and drop, using a slider to change data, calculations performed only by the client and which do not need to be sent back to the server, for example, a mortgage calculator.

— *More responsive.* The interface behaviors are typically much more responsive than those of a standard Web browser that must always interact with a remote server.

The most sophisticated examples of RIAs exhibit a look and feel approaching that of a desktop environment. Using a client engine can also produce other performance benefits:

— *Client/Server balance.* The demand for client and server computing resources is better balanced, so that the Web server need not be the workhorse that it is with a traditional Web application. This frees server resources, allowing the same server hardware to handle more client sessions concurrently.

— *Asynchronous communication.* The client engine can interact with the server asynchronously — that is, without waiting for the user to perform an interface action like clicking on a button or link. This option allows RIA designers to move data between the client and the server without making the user wait. Perhaps the most common application of this is prefetching, in which an application anticipates a future need for certain data, and downloads it to the client before the user requests it, thereby speeding up a subsequent response. Google Maps uses this technique to move adjacent map segments to the client before the user scrolls their view.

— *Network efficiency*. The network traffic may also be significantly reduced because an application-specific client engine can be more intelligent than a standard Web browser when deciding what data needs to be exchanged with servers. This can speed up individual requests or responses because less data is being transferred for each interaction, and overall network load is reduced. However, use of asynchronous prefetching techniques can neutralize or even reverse this potential benefit. Because the code cannot anticipate exactly what every user will do next, it is common for such techniques to download extra data, not all of which is actually needed, to many or all clients.

Shortcomings and Restrictions

Shortcomings and restrictions associated with RIAs are:

— *Sandbox*. Because RIAs run within a sandbox, they have restricted access to system resources. If assumptions about access to resources are incorrect, RIAs may fail to operate correctly.

— *Disabled scripting*. JavaScript or another scripting language is often required. If the user has disabled active scripting in their browser, the RIA may not function properly, if at all.

— *Client processing speed*. To achieve platform independence, some RIAs use client-side scripts written in interpreted languages such as JavaScript, with a consequential loss of performance. This is not an issue with compiled client languages such as Java, where performance is comparable to that of traditional compiled languages, or with Flash movies, in which the bulk of the operations are performed by the native code of the Flash player.

— *Script download time.* Although it does not have to be installed, the additional client-side intelligence (or client engine) of RIA applications needs to be delivered by the server to the client. While much of this is usually automatically cached it needs to be transferred at least once. Depending on the size and type of delivery, script download time may be unpleasantly long. RIA developers can lessen the impact of this delay by compressing the scripts, and by staging their delivery over multiple pages of an application.

— *Loss of integrity.* If the application-base is X/HTML, conflicts arise between the goal of an application (which naturally wants to be in control of its presentation and behaviour) and the goals of X/HTML (which naturally wants to give away control). The DOM interface for X/HTML makes it possible to create RIAs, but by doing so makes it impossible to guarantee correct function. Because an RIA client can modify the RIA's basic structure and override presentation and behaviour, it can cause an irrecoverable client failure or crash. Eventually, this problem could be solved by new client-side mechanisms that granted an RIA client more limited permission to modify only those resources within the scope of its application. (Standard software running natively does not have this problem because by definition a program automatically possesses all rights to all its allocated resources).

— *Loss of visibility to search engines.* Search engines may not be able to index the text content of the application.

— *Dependence on an Internet connection.* While the ideal network-enabled replacement for a desktop application would allow users to be "occasionally connected" wandering in and out of hot-spots or from office to office, today the typical RIA requires network connectivity.

Management Complications

The advent of RIA technologies has introduced considerable additional complexity into Web applications. Traditional Web applications built using only standard HTML, having a relatively simple software architecture and being constructed using a limited set of development options, are relatively easy to design and manage. For the person or organization using RIA technologies to deliver a Web application, their additional complexity makes them harder to design, test, measure, and support.

Use of RIA technology poses several new Service Level Management ("SLM") challenges, not all of which are completely solved today. SLM concerns are not always the focus of application developers, and are rarely if ever perceived by application users, but they are vital to the successful delivery of an online application. Aspects of the RIA architecture that complicate management processes are:

— Greater complexity makes development harder. The ability to move code to the client gives application designers and developers far more creative freedom. But this in turn makes development harder, increases the likelihood of defects (bugs) being introduced, and complicates software testing activities. These complications lengthen the software development process, regardless of the particular methodology or process being employed. Some of these issues may be mitigated through the use of a Web application framework to standardize aspects of RIA design and development. However, increasing complexity in a software solution can complicate and lengthen the testing process, if it increases the number of use cases to be tested. Incomplete testing lowers the application's quality and its reliability during use. One could argue that the above comment applies not specifically to RIA technology, but to complexity in general. For example, that exact same argument was used when Apple and Microsoft independently announced the GUI in the 1980s, and perhaps even when Ford announced the Model T. Nonetheless, humans have shown a remarkable ability to absorb technological advances for decades, if not centuries.

— RIA architecture breaks the Web page paradigm. Traditional Web applications can be viewed as a series of Web pages, each of which requires a distinct download, initiated by an HTTP GET request. This model has been characterized as the Web page paradigm. RIAs invalidate this model, introducing additional asynchronous server communications to support a more responsive user interface. In RIAs, the time to complete a page download may no longer correspond to something a user perceives as important, because (for example) the client engine may be prefetching some of the downloaded content for future use. New measurement techniques must be devised for RIAs, to permit reporting of response time quantities that reflect the user's experience. In the absence of standard tools that do this, RIA developers must instrument their application code to produce the measurement data needed for SLM.

— Asynchronous communication makes it harder to isolate performance problems. Paradoxically, actions taken to enhance application responsiveness also make it harder to measure, understand, report on, and manage responsiveness. Some RIAs do not issue any further HTTP GET requests from the browser after their first page, using asynchronous requests from the client engine to initiate all subsequent downloads. The RIA client engine may be programmed to continually download new content and refresh the display, or (in applications using the Comet approach) a server-side engine can keep pushing new content to the browser over a connection that never closes. In these cases, the concept of a "page download" is no longer applicable. These complications make it harder to measure and subdivide application response times, a fundamental requirement for problem isolation and service level management. Tools designed to measure traditional Web applications may — depending on the details of the application and the tool — report such applications either as a single Web page per HTTP request, or as an unrelated collection of server activities. Neither conclusion reflects what is really happening at the application level.

— The client engine makes it harder to measure response time. For traditional Web applications, measurement software can reside either on the client machine or on a machine that is close to the server, provided that it can observe the flow of network traffic at the TCP and HTTP levels. Because these protocols are synchronous and predictable, a packet sniffer can read and interpret packet-level data, and infer the user's experience of response time by tracking HTTP messages and the times of underlying TCP packets and acknowledgments. But the RIA architecture reduces the power of the packet sniffing approach, because the client engine breaks the communication between user and server into two separate cycles operating asynchronously — a foreground (user-to-engine) cycle, and a background (engine-to-server) cycle. Both cycles are important, because neither stands alone; it is their relationship that defines application behavior. But that relationship depends only on the application design, which cannot (in general) be inferred by a measurement tool, especially one that can observe only one of the two cycles. Therefore the most complete RIA measurements can only be obtained using tools that reside on the client and observe both cycles.

Development and Adoption of RIA

RIAs are still in the early stages of development and user adoption. There are a number of restrictions and requirements that remain:

— *Browser adoption*: Many RIAs require modern web browsers in order to run. Advanced JavaScript engines must be present in the browser as RIAs use techniques such as XMLHTTPRequest for client-server communication, and DOM Scripting and advanced CSS techniques to enable the rich user interface.

— *Web standards*: Differences between web browsers can make it difficult to write an RIA that will run across all major browsers. The consistency of the Java platform, particularly after Java 1.1, makes this task much simpler for RIAs written as Java applets.

— *Development tools*: Some Ajax Frameworks and products such as Curl, Adobe Flex and Microsoft Silverlight provide an integrated environment in which to build RIAs.

— *Accessibility concerns*: Additional interactivity may require technical approaches that limit applications' accessibility.

— *User adoption*: Users expecting standard web applications may find that some accepted browser functionality may have somewhat different or even undesired behaviour.

Justifications

Although developing applications to run in a web browser is a much more limiting, difficult, and intricate a process than developing a regular desktop application, the efforts are often justified because:

- installation is not required — updating and distributing the application is an instant, automatically handled process
- updates/upgrades to new versions are automatic
- users can use the application from any computer with an internet connection, and usually regardless of what operating system that computer is running
- web-based applications are generally less prone to viral infection than running an actual executable
- as web usage increases, computer users are becoming less willing to go to the trouble of installing new software if a browser-based alternative is available

This last point is often true even if this alternative is slower or not as feature-rich.

Methods and Techniques

JavaScript

The first major client side language and technology available with the ability to run code and installed on a majority of web clients was JavaScript. Although its uses were relatively limited at first, combined with layers and other developments in DHTML it has become possible to piece together an RIA system without the use of a unified client-side solution. Ajax is a new term coined to refer to this combination of techniques and has recently been used most prominently by Google for projects such as Gmail and Google Maps. However, creating a large application in this framework is very difficult, as many different technologies must interact to make it work, and browser compatibility requires a lot of effort. In order to make the process easier, several open source Ajax Frameworks have been developed, as well as commercial frameworks.

Adobe Flash

Adobe Flash is another way to build Rich Internet Applications. This technology is cross-platform and quite powerful to create an application UI. Adobe Flex provides the option to create Flash user interface by compiling MXML, a XML based interface description language. Adobe is currently working on providing a more powerful platform with the product Adobe AIR, a technology combining HTMLs (including Ajax applications) Flash player based applications and PDFs.

OpenLaszlo

OpenLaszlo is an open source rich Internet application framework developed by Laszlo Systems Inc.. The OpenLaszlo server compiles programs written in the LZX language (a mixture of XML tags and JavaScript) into either DHTML (commonly known as AJAX now) or Adobe Flash bytecode, currently supporting Flash7 and Flash8. The server - which originally was a proprietary software - was open sourced in October 2004 under the Common Public License. OpenLaszlo is the only rich Internet application platform which is capable of compiling into two different runtimes from the same code base.

Windows Presentation Foundation and Silverlight

With the .NET 3.0 Framework, Microsoft introduced

Windows Presentation Foundation (WPF) which provides a way to build single-platform applications with some similarities to RIAs using XAML and languages like C# and Visual Basic. In addition, Microsoft has announced Silverlight, which may eventually provide a subset of WPF functionality on devices and other platforms.

ActiveX Controls

Embedding ActiveX controls into HTML is a very powerful way to develop rich Internet applications, however they are only guaranteed to run properly in Internet Explorer. Furthermore, since they can break the sandbox model, they are potential targets for computer viruses and malware making them high security risks. At the time of this writing, the Adobe Flash Player for Internet Explorer is implemented as an ActiveX control for Microsoft environments, as well as in multi-platform Netscape Plugin wrappers for the wider world. Only if corporations have standardized on using Internet Explorer as the primary web browser, is ActiveX per se a good choice for building corporate applications.

Curl 5.0, Rebol 2.6 and Seaside for Smalltalk

Alternatives to Java and the JVM for RIA are not lacking: three alternative abstract machines are available in the form of the Curl, Rebol and Smalltalk. Curl facilitates Client-side persistent data, Rebol does not require a browser and Seaside for Smalltalk uses a minor extension to Smalltalk to provide a much richer web experience. All three alternatives are far more mature than more familiar options and as old or older than Java and the JVM.

JavaFX

Sun Microsystems has announced JavaFX, a family of products based on Java technology designed to provide a consistent experience across a wide variety of devices including desktops, (as applets and stand-alone clients) set-top boxes, mobile devices, and Blu-Ray players. The JavaFX platform will initially comprise JavaFX Script and JavaFX Mobile. Invented by Sun Software Engineer Chris Oliver as a skunk works project, JavaFX Script enables rapid development of rich 2D interfaces using a declarative syntax similar to SVG. Sun plans to release JavaFX Script as an open source project, but JavaFX Mobile will be a commercial product available through an OEM license to carriers and handset manufacturers.

Java Applets

Java applets run in standard HTML pages and generally start automatically when their web page is opened with a modern web browser. Java applets have access to the screen (inside an area designated in its page's HTML), as well as the speakers, keyboard and mouse of any computer their web page is opened on, as well as access to the Internet, and provide a sophisticated environment capable of real time applications.

Java Applications

Java based RIAs can be launched from within the browser or as free standing applications via Java Web Start. Java RIAs can take advantage of the full power of the Java platform to deliver rich functionality, 2D & 3D graphics, and off-line capabilities, but at the cost of delayed startup.

Numerous frameworks for Java RIAs exist, including XUL-like XML-based frameworks such as XUI, Swixml, or Canoo's thin Swing-approach, UltraLightClient.

User Interface Languages

As an alternative to HTML/XHTML new user interface markup languages can be used in RIAs. For instance, the

Mozilla Foundation's XML-based user interface markup language XUL - this could be used in RIAs though it would be restricted to Mozilla-based browsers, since it is not a de facto or de jure standard. The W3C's Rich Web Clients Activity has initiated a Web Application Formats Working Group whose mission includes the development of such standards. The original DARPA project at MIT which resulted in the W3C also resulted in the the web content language Curl which is now in version 5.0.

RIA's user interfaces can also become richer through the use of scriptable SVG (though not all browsers support native SVG rendering yet) as well as SMIL.

Other Techniques

RIAs could use XForms to enhance their functionality. Using XML and XSLT along with some XHTML, CSS and JavaScript can also be used to generate richer client side UI components like data tables that can be resorted locally on the client without going back to the server. Mozilla and Internet Explorer browsers both support this. The Omnis Web Client is an ActiveX control or Netscape plug-in which can be embedded into an HTML page providing a rich application interface in the end-user's web browser.

RIA with Real-time Push

Traditionally, web pages have been delivered to the client only when the client requested for it. For every client request, the browser initiates an HTTP connection to the web server, which then returns the data and the connection is closed. The drawback of this approach was that the page displayed was updated only when the user explicitly refreshes the page or moves to a new page. Since transferring entire pages can take a long time, refreshing pages can introduce a long latency.

Demand for Localised Usage of RIA

With the increasing adoption and improvement in broadband technologies, fewer users experience poor performance caused by remote latency. Furthermore one of the critical reasons for using an RIA is that many developers are looking for a language to serve up desktop applications that is not only desktop OS neutral but also installation and system issue free.

RIA running in the ubiquitous web browser is a potential candidate even when used standalone or over a LAN, with the required webserver functionalities hosted locally.

5

Web Operating Systems

Web operating system and WebOS are terms that describe network services for internet scale distributed computing, as in the WebOS Project at UC Berkeley , and the WOS Project . In both cases the scale of the web operating system extends across the internet, like the web. However, the terms WebOS and Web operating system have been employed more broadly and with far greater popularity in the context of "the web as in HTTP", and for many meanings ranging from singular systems to collections of systems .

Common to all uses, a Web operating system is distinct from Internet operating systems in that it is independent of the traditional individual computer operating system. This conception of the system reflects an evolution of research in the field of operating systems into the increasingly minimized (for example, TinyOS and Exokernel) and distributed (for example, Inferno), and for distributed systems increasingly defined in terms of the specification of their network protocols more than their implementations.

There's an ongoing controversy upon whether the new breed of WebOSs, that include eyeOS (which is Open Source), Oos, YouOS, G.ho.st, DesktopTwo and eXo

WebOS are actually OSs that fall within the broad definition of the term . The fact that all of these new WebOSs run over a browser window and/or a plugin and have no relation whatsoever with the hardware and its drivers seems to be central to this discussion. According to some of the people that actually run one of these sites, the object of these sites is to turn the desktop itself into a service that runs on the Internet rather than on the local OS. So the term 'web desktop' or 'webtop' may seem more appropriate to some. On the other hand, as these services start to include a file system, application management systems and so on, they do overlap more and more with the typical functionality of an OS.

A Web operating system, could also be defined as operating system that solely provides Web access. Web operating systems like these have been known as kiosks. However since the paradigm of Web computing is not limited to kiosk environments, a broader definition of a "Web operating system" is apt.

WebOS Project

The WebOS Project is a computing research project started at the University of California, Berkeley to develop suitable software development abstractions for applications that run over a network. The abstractions it provides include:

- a filesystem that identifies data by uniform resource locators
- a location-independent resource naming system
- secure remote execution
- secure data access
- fail-safe transactions

Research on WebOS has continued at Duke University, the University of Texas at Austin, and the University of Washington. The conception of the web operating system in the WebOS project can be characterized as a finite or catalogued collection of services.

History of WebOS

WebOS gained popularity in 1999 when a much touted start up, WebOS Inc. (at first known as Hyperoffice and later known as MyWebOS), was founded by Berkeley grad Shervin Pishevar and Emory grad Drew Morris. WebOS licensed the WebOS technologies from Duke University and University of Texas (Austin) and recruited Dr. Amin Vahdat, Professor of Computer Science at Duke, who had pioneered the WebOS technologies at University of California at Berkeley where he got his PhD on his WebOS research.

WebOS acquired WebOS.org, which was created by a young Swedish programmer, Fredrik Malmer, who had created the first online desktop environment. Soon after, some of the top DHTML and Javascript programmers in the world such as Erik Arvidsson of WebFx fame, Dan Steinman, creator of the Dynamic Duo Cross-browser DHTML API, joined WebOS. WebOS raised over $10 million in financing from Impact Venture Partners led by Adam Dell and Grotech Capital.

WebOS was launched with a vision of creating the first web operating system complete with a WebOS API allowing developers to create Windows-like web applications that worked an extremely fast speeds by caching much of the code in the local browser. Arvidsson later launched Bindows, a framework very similar to the WebOS API, that does much of this and is used by many large companies and the US Military. WebOS filed the very first WebOS patents in 1999. WebOS competed with another start up, Desktop.com, which was aimed more at the consumer market. WebOS was covered by many media outlets such as the Wall Street Journal, financial Times, LA Times, Power lunch on CNBC, Fox News and CNN and helped spread the meme further. WebOS launched Hyperoffice, a full office suite, back in 1999.

TYPES OF WEB PPERATING SYSTEM

Desktoptwo

Desktoptwo is a Webtop or WebOS developed by Sapotek that mimics the look, feel and functionality of the desktop environment of an operating system. The software is currently in beta stage yet has acquired over 120,000 active users since its launch in August 2006. Desktoptwo is fully web-based and requires Flash player to operate.

Unlike some other so-called online desktops, which are more akin to aggregators of stand-alone applications, the web applications found on Desktoptwo are built on the same open source scripting language, PHP, and as a result the applications are interoperable and include, for example, drag-and-drop functionality. Sapotek has also created a Spanish language version of Desktoptwo called Computadora.de and is the sponsor of a free software community, Sapodesk, through which it has liberated all the web applications found on Desktoptwo and works with community members to create additional open source web applications.

Some of its features are:

— File sharing

— Webmail

— Blog creator

— Instant messenger

— Address book

— Calendar

— Live Chat rooms

— Notepad

— Bookmarks/Favorites

— Message boards

— RSS Reader

— Website Editor

— Office productivity applications

— Online document collaboration

Dewspot

The dewspot is a multi-lingual Ajax-based configurable mashup application. It is organized into desktops, with each desktop containing windows. Now dewspot include weather forecasts, Flickr photos, Google map, YouTube videos, Twitter micro-blogging windows. A desktop can be configured further by using of one of many existing themes and wallpapers.

eXo WebOS

eXo WebOS is a web desktop which is also available for download as open source software (GPL), and allows everyone to install their own eXo WebOS server.

Public APIs are available all over the place and many Ajax-based mash-up services are reusing them to build rich client solutions inside the browser. So far, portals have tried to aggregate services inside a coherent and secure personalized place but were limited to Web 1.0 technologies.

eXo Platform is a set of products that allows to tie together the web and the desktop, the enterprise and consumer digital lives in a coherent platform on which people can build efficient applications such as Contact Managements, Calendars, Business intelligence, CRM, Document Management Systems and many others.

But with eXo you of course have one entry point to get all this but you also get a unique UI that looks like what people are familiar with in their usual desktop environment. Note that in the same site it is also possible to have more usual layouts pages where applications are displayed in columns or rows.

Furthermore, the User Interface is just a part of the whole system . The entire platform is bult upon standards that make it inter operable with huge number of external applications.

eyeOS

eyeOS is an open source (GPL) web operating system. It provides a default desktop with some base applications and the ability of developing new applications with the eyeOS Toolkit, the integrated IDE, which can be installed through the ports-based eyeSoft system. This allows anyone to create their own repository for eyeOS and distribute their eyeOS Applications automatically to its users. The idea behind eyeOS is to provide a full operating system, web based, which can be accessed from everywhere, with any Internet-capable device.

eyeOS 0.6.0 (first version available) was released at August 1, 2005. After two years, the eyeOS Team published eyeOS 1.0 (at June 4, 2007). eyeOS 1.0 introduced some new web technologies, like eyeSoft, a ports-based web software installation system (like apt-get for Debian based Linux distributions), and the eyeOS Toolkit, to develop Web Applications easily. At July 2, 2007, eyeOS 1.1 was released. and eyeOS changed its license from GNU GPL Version 2 to Version 3.

GCOE X

GCOE X is a Web desktop developed by Vista Enterprises that gives users a full featured Desktop Environment in any modern Web Browser capable of running JavaScript. GCOE X is currently still in development

G.ho.st

G.ho.st (usually pronounced ghost) is the trading name of Ghost Inc. and the service name and URL of the company's hosted computer operating system or WebOS service. Its name is an acronym of Global Hosted Operating SysTem. It provides, ove- the internet, a working environment that mimics the classic desktop provided by personal computer operating systems. As an internet based service, users are able to create, save and return to a working environment from different physical computers. G.ho.st calls itself a Virtual Computer. In April 2007 the software entered alpha stage development, and as of July 2007 it remains in this stage.

Such services are not considered operating systems in the traditional sense although they are sometimes referred to as Web Operating Systems. Whilst they can include a GUI (e.g. a desktop), a (virtual) file system, application management and security, they do not contain a kernel to interface with physical hardware. Therefore, to use the service an operating system is required, from which the service can be run.

OOS

OOS (short for Online Operating System) is a web desktop developed by iCUBE. It is available at www.oos.cc for free usage. The OOS is similar to WebOS's such as YouOS and other so-called "web operating systems" or "webtops". A webtop offers several advantages over standard desktops used on a PC like the ability to own a personalized desktop on every PC which has a simple internet browser installed.

The interface of OOS much appears a "clone" of that of Microsoft Windows 2000, even more so than how ReactOS does of Windows NT.

The central features of the OOS can be summarized as follows:

— *General*: The Online Operating System is being developed with the aim of providing a "maximum level of usability in the World Wide Web" . It therefore provides comprehensive support of drag and drop, a well-known look & feel as well as an appealing user interface.

— *Multi-Language Support*: All the applications of the Online Operating System can be easily translated into any other language. Currently English and German versions of all applications are available.

— *Theme Support*: The look of the OOS can be adapted by use of different themes. Currently, three different themes are included, further skins can be created based on CSS and Images.

Applications

The current set of applications is currently available in the Online Operating System:

— *File Manager:* Upload, download and manage files online: 1 GB of free web space is currently included.

— *File Sharing:* Via the file manager it is possible to share files with other users of the OOS.

— *Web Browser:* Open web documents in the OOS internal browser.

— *Write*: Open, view and edit formatted documents.

— *Editor:* Open, view and edit text as well as HTML documents.

— *Image viewer:* View images directly within the internal image viewing utility: Also a full-screen mode is available.

— *Media Player:* View movies and listen to MP3 music, directly within the Online Operating System.

— *PDF Viewer*: Open PDF documents within the OOS.

— *Calculator*: Perform simple calculations.

— *Games*: Various Flash-based games are available: Currently a Mario game as well as a funny cow game are included.

— *Display Settings*: Change the skin of the desktop, background image and background color, etc.

— *Web Publishing:* Publish a web page or a photo album with only a few clicks directly from within the OOS. A subdomain and free webspace is included for free.

— *Profile Management:* Manage the user's profile information, including spoken languages, contact details, etc.

— *Application Management:* Manage the set of available applications, desktop as well as quicklaunch links.

— *Feedback Agent:* Report bugs and communicate with the developers of the OOS.

— *Tip of the Day:* Learn more about the central features of the OOS.

— *Groupware Suite*: A comprehensive suite such as Microsoft Outlook shall be created, consisting of at least the following elements:

— *Mail:* Send and receive mail messages directly within the Online Operating System.

— *Calendar*: Manage an individual calendar online.

— *Todos:* Manage simple tasks.

— *Notes:* Remember important information by storing them on post-it notes.

— *Developer's Studio:* Create and execute own OOS applications.

All applications provided in OOS are written entirely in JavaScript by using the (proprietary) reBOX API. This API is commercial whereas the provided applications themselves are published open source. Soon it will be possible for developers to actively participate in the creation of OOS applications. For this purpose, a development environment will be available which makes it possible to create, execute and publish own applications for oneself and the other users of the Online Operating System. The set of provided open source applications shall provide a good starting point in the respective development processes.

XinDesk

Xindesk is a free WebOS that runs in a web browser. It requires a web browser with JavaScript support. It is developed by the XIN company, based in Sweden. The product is built on the technical foundation of Xin teleport.

Some of its features are:

— Address book

— Calendar

— E-mail accounts

— File explorer

— Games

— Instant messenger

YouOS

YouOS is an experimental web desktop produced by WebShaka, that replicates the desktop environment of a modern operating system on a webpage, using JavaScript to communicate with the remote server. This allows users to save the current desktop state to return to later, much like the hibernation feature in many true operating systems, and for multiple users to collaborate using a single environment. YouOS features built-in sharing of music, documents and other files. The software is currently in alpha stage, and is referred to as a "web operating system" by WebShaka. An application programming interface has been created by WebShaka, and an IDE (integrated development environment) is in development. Over 700 applications have been created using this API.

WEB PORTAL

A web portal is a site that functions as a point of access to information on the World Wide Web. Portals present information from diverse sources in a unified way. Popular portals are MSN, Yahoo, and AOL. Aside from the search engine standard, web portals offer other services such as news, stock prices, infotainment and various other features. Portals provide a way for enterprises to provide a consistent look and feel with access control and procedures for multiple applications, which otherwise would have been different entities altogether.

A personal portal is a site on the World Wide Web that typically provides personalized capabilities to its visitors, providing a pathway to other content. It is designed to use distributed applications, different numbers and types of middleware and hardware to provide services from a number of different sources. In addition, business portals are designed to share collaboration in workplaces. A further business-driven requirement of portals is that the content be able to work on multiple platforms such as personal computers, personal digital assistants (PDAs), and cell phones.

It is often necessary to have a centralized application that has access to various other applications within the same enterprise to share the information across the applications. Also the various users with different roles accessing the different applications prefer to have a single access point to all of them over the Internet. They like to personalize the applications and have the coupled applications coordinated. Above all, the administrator users like to have administrative tools all in a single place to administer all the applications. All these are achieved through portals. Since all the applications share information through portals, there is better communication between various types of users. Another advantage of portals is that they can make event-driven campaigns. Below is detailed list of advantages of using portals:

— Intelligent integration and access to enterprise content, applications and processes

— Improved communication and collaboration among customers, partners, and employees

— Unified, real-time access to information held in disparate systems

— Personalized user interactions

— Rapid, easy modification and maintenance of the website presentation

— Below are the properties of portals:

— Look and feel

— Consistent headers and footers, color schemes, icons and logos which gives the user a feel and sense of consistency, uniformity, and ease of navigation

— A portlet is an application within a browser window, displayed in an effective layout

— A portlet is itself a web application

— Portlets are aggregated by the portal page

Development of Personal Portals

In the late 1990s, the web portal was a hot commodity. After the proliferation of web browsers in the mid-1990s, many companies tried to build or acquire a portal, to have a piece of the Internet market. The web portal gained special attention because it was, for many users, the starting point of their web browser. Netscape became a part of America Online, the Walt Disney Company launched Go.com, and Excite and @Home became a part of AT&T during the late 1990s. Lycos was said to be a good target for other media companies such as CBS.

Many of the portals started initially as either web directories (notably Yahoo!) and/or search engines (Excite, Lycos, AltaVista, infoseek, and Hotbot among the old ones). Expanding services was a strategy to secure the user-base and lengthen the time a user stayed on the portal. Services which require user registration such as free email, customization features, and chatrooms were considered to enhance repeat use of the portal. Game, chat, email, news, and other services also tend to make users stay longer, thereby increasing the advertising revenue.

The portal craze, with "old media" companies racing to outbid each other for Internet properties, died down with the dot-com flameout in 2000 and 2001. Disney pulled the plug on Go.com, Excite went bankrupt and its remains were sold to iWon.com. Some notable portal sites Yahoo!, for instance, remain successful to this day. To modern dot-com businesses, the portal craze serves as a cautionary tale about the risks of rushing into a market crowded with highly-capitalized but largely undifferentiated me-too companies.

Regional Web Portals

Along with the development and success of international personal portals such as Yahoo!, regional variants have also sprung up. Some regional portals contain local information such as weather forecasts, street maps and local business information. Another notable expansion over the past couple of years is the move into formerly unthinkable markets.

"Local content - global reach" portals have emerged not only from countries like Korea (Naver.com), India (Rediff), China (Sina.com), Romania(Neogen.ro), Greece(in.gr) and Italy (Webplace.it), but in countries like Vietnam where they are very important for learning how to apply e-commerce, e-government, etc. Such portals reach out to the widespread diaspora across the world.

Government web portals

At the end of the dot-com boom in the 1990s, many governments had already committed to creating portal sites for their citizens. In the United States the main portal is USA.gov, in addition to portals developed for specific audiences such as DisabilityInfo.gov; in the United Kingdom the main portals are Directgov (for citizens) and businesslink.gov.uk (for businesses).

Many U.S. states have their own portals which provide direct access to eCommerce applications (e.g., Hawaii Business Express and myIndianaLicense), agency and department web sites, and more specific information about living in, doing business in and getting around the state.

Many U.S. states have chosen to out-source the operation of their portals to third-party vendors. One company that is an example of this is NICUSA which runs 20 state portals.

One of the issues that comes up with government web portals is that different agencies often have their own portals and sometimes a statewide portal-directory structure is not sophisticated and deep enough to meet the needs of multiple agencies. Over the last few years more sophisticated technologies are allowing loosely-coupled portal integrations bound together by standard interoperability formats (like SIF) that support a more heterogeneous non-parallel environment.

Corporate Web Portals

Corporate intranets gained popularity during the 1990s. Having access to a variety of company information via a web browser was a new way of working. Intranets quickly grew in size and complexity, and webmasters (many of whom lacked the discipline of managing content and users) became overwhelmed in their duties. It wasn't enough to have a consolidated view of company information, users were demanding personalization and customization. Webmasters, if skilled enough, were able to offer some capabilities, but for the most part ended up driving users away from using the intranet.

The 1990s were a time of innovation for the concept of corporate web portals. Many companies began to offer tools to help webmasters manage their data, applications and information more easily, and through personalized views. Some portal solutions today are able to integrate legacy applications, other portals objects, and handle thousands of user requests.

Today's corporate portals are sprouting new value-added capabilities for businesses. Capabilities such as managing workflows, increasing collaboration between work groups, and allowing content creators to self-publish their information are lifting the burden off already strapped IT departments.

In addition, most portal solutions today, if architected correctly, can allow internal and external access to specific corporate information using secure authentication or Single-Sign-On.

JSR168 Standards emerged around 2001. Java Specification Request (JSR) 168 standards allow the interoperability of portlets across different portal platforms. These standards allow portal developers, administrators and consumers to integrate standards-based portals and portlets across a variety of vendor solutions.

Microsoft's SharePoint Portal Server line of products have been gaining popularity among corporations for building their portals, partly due to the tight integration with the rest of the Microsoft Office products. Research by Forrester Research in 2004 shows that Microsoft is the vendor of choice for companies looking for portal server software.

In response to Microsoft's strong presence in the portal market, other portal vendors are being acquired, or are challenging their offering. Oracle Corporation, in 2007, released Web Center Suite, a similar product to SharePoint. Web Center Suite has a full line of collaboration tools (blogs, wikis, team spaces, calendaring, email, etc.).

In addition, the popularity of content aggregation is growing and portal solution will continue to evolve significantly over the next few years. The Gartner Group predicts generation 8 portals to expand on the enterprise mash-up concept of delivering a variety of information, tools, applications and access points through a single mechanism.

With the increase in user generated content, disparate data silo's, and file formats, information architects and taxonomist will be required to allow users the ability to tag (classify) the data. This will ultimately cause a ripple effect where users will also be generating adhoc navigation and information flows.

Hosted Web Portals

As corporate portals gained popularity a number of companies began offering them as a hosted service. The hosted portal market fundamentally changed the composition of portals. In many ways they served simply as a tool for publishing information instead of the loftier goals of integrating legacy applications or presenting correlated data from distributed databases. The early hosted portal companies such as Hyperoffice.com or the now defunct InternetPortal.com focused on collaboration and scheduling in addition to the distribution of corporate data. As hosted web portals have risen in popularity their feature set has grown to include hosted databases, document management, email, discussion forums and more. Hosted portals automatically personalize the content generated from their modules to provide a personalized experience to their users. In this regard they have remained true to the original goals of the earlier corporate web portals.

Domain specific portals

A number of portals have come about that are specific to a particular domain, offering access to related companies and services, a prime example of this trend would be the growth in property portals that give access to services such as estate agents, removal firm and solicitors that offer conveyancing. Examples of this type of portal would be TheBigMover.com (Spain), rightmove.co.uk (UK), trulia.com (US).

Web Desktop

A web desktop or webtop is a network application system for integrating web applications into a web based work space. It is a virtual desktop on the web, running in a web browser as software. Web desktops often are characterized by an environment similar to that of Windows, Mac, or Linux, but are now considered to have much more functionality being dependent on the internet. Typical benefits include the ability to save work and settings over the internet rather than to the local desktop.

The term Webtop was first introduced by the Santa Cruz Operation (SCO) in 1993 for a web-based interface to their UNIX operating system. Andy Bovingdon and Ronald Record, who both explored the concepts in different directions, are often credited as the inventors. The initial concept was launched as the Tarantella Webtop. This technology originated from early commercial use of web server technology by SCO (SCO was the first OS vendor to include a commercial web server), their

X.desktop product line (obtained when they acquired IXI Limited in the UK, which was the first to have icons for URLs and an HTML-based help system). Tarantella allowed real UNIX and Windows applications to be displayed within a web browser through the use of Java to form a true web based desktop or Webtop.

The first SCO Webtop releases were part of SCO Skunkworks before being integrated into OpenServer version 5 and UnixWare 7. Byte magazine referred to the Webtop as a NUI (Network User Interface).

Nivio then took a full windows desktop with full user ability to installs applications on demand on a monthly rental and put it online with an offline device as well if the user never had a physical machine; the Nivio Platform was the first Desktop-over-IP that allowed users to actually be able to move from the traditional PC model.

6

Web Browsers

A Web browser is a software application that enables a user to display and interact with text, images, and other information typically located on a Web page at a website on the World Wide Web or a local area network. Text and images on a Web page can contain hyperlinks to other Web pages at the same or different website. Web browsers allow a user to quickly and easily access information provided on many Web pages at many websites by traversing these links. Web browsers format HTML information for display, so the appearance of a Web page may differ between browsers.

Some of the Web browsers available for personal computers include Internet Explorer, Mozilla Firefox, Safari, Opera, and Netscape in order of descending popularity (in August 2006). Web browsers are the most commonly used type of HTTP user agent. Although browsers are typically used to access the World Wide Web, they can also be used to access information provided by Web servers in private networks or content in file systems.

Protocols and Standards

Web browsers communicate with Web servers primarily using HTTP (hypertext transfer protocol) to fetch webpages. HTTP allows Web browsers to submit information to Web servers as well as fetch Web pages from them. The most commonly used HTTP is HTTP/1.1, which is fully defined in RFC 2616. HTTP/1.1 has its own required standards that Internet Explorer does not fully support, but most other current-generation Web browsers do.

Pages are located by means of a URL (uniform resource locator, RFC 1738), which is treated as an address, beginning with http: for HTTP access. Many browsers also support a variety of other URL types and their corresponding protocols, such as gopher: for Gopher (a hierarchical hyperlinking protocol), ftp: for FTP (file transfer protocol), rtsp: for RTSP (real-time streaming protocol), and https: for HTTPS (an SSL encrypted version of HTTP).

The file format for a Web page is usually HTML (hyper-text markup language) and is identified in the HTTP protocol using a MIME content type. Most browsers natively support a variety of formats in addition to HTML, such as the JPEG, PNG and GIF image formats, and can be extended to support more through the use of plugins. The combination of HTTP content type and URL protocol specification allows Web page designers to embed images, animations, video, sound, and streaming media into a Web page, or to make them accessible through the Web page.

Early Web browsers supported only a very simple version of HTML. The rapid development of proprietary Web browsers led to the development of non-standard dialects of HTML, leading to problems with Web interoperability. Modern Web browsers support a combination of standards- and defacto-based HTML and XHTML, which should display in the same way across all browsers. No browser fully supports HTML 4.01, XHTML

1.x or CSS 2.1 yet. Currently many sites are designed using WYSIWYG HTML generation programs such as Macromedia Dreamweaver or Microsoft FrontPage. These often generate non-standard HTML by default, hindering the work of the W3C in developing standards, specifically with XHTML and CSS (cascading style sheets, used for page layout).

Some of the more popular browsers include additional components to support Usenet news, IRC (Internet relay chat), and e-mail. Protocols supported may include NNTP (network news transfer protocol), SMTP (simple mail transfer protocol), IMAP (Internet message access protocol), and POP (post office protocol). These browsers are often referred to as Internet suites or application suites rather than merely Web browsers.

History of Web Browsers

A NeXTcube was used by Tim Berners-Lee (who pioneered the use of hypertext for sharing information) as the world's first Web server, and also an early Web browser, WorldWideWeb in 1990. Berners-Lee introduced it to colleagues at CERN in March 1991. Since then the development of Web browsers has been inseparably intertwined with the development of the Web itself.

The first browser, Silversmith, was created by John Bottoms in 1987. The browser, based on SGML tags, used a tag set from the Electronic Document Project of the AAP with minor modifications and was sold to a number of early adopters. At the time SGML was used exclusively for the formatting of printed documents. The use of SGML for electronically displayed documents signaled a shift in electronic publishing and was met with considerable resistance. Silversmith included an integrated indexer, full text searches, hypertext links between images text and sound using SGML tags and a return stack for use with hypertext links. It included features that are still not available in today's browsers. These include capabilities such as the ability to restrict searches within document structures, searches on indexed documents using wild cards and the ability to search on tag attribute values and attribute names. SGML-FAQ US Patent

In April 1990, a draft patent application for a mass market consumer device for browsing pages via links "PageLink" was proposed by Craig Cockburn at Digital Equipment Co Ltd (DEC) whilst working in their Networking and Communications division in Reading, England. This application for a keyboardless touch screen browser for consumers also makes reference to "navigating and searching text" and "bookmarks" was aimed at (quotes paraphrased) "replacing books", "storing a shopping list" "have an updated personalised newspaper updated round the clock", "dynamically updated maps for use in a car" and suggests such a device could have a "profound effect on the advertising industry". The patent was canned by Digital as too futuristic and being largely hardware based had obstacles to market that purely software driven approaches did not suffer from.

In 1992, Tony Johnson releases the MidasWWW browser. Based on Motif/X, MidasWWW allows viewing of PostScript files on the Web from Unix and VMS, and even handles compressed PostScript.

Another early popular Web browser was ViolaWWW, which was modeled after HyperCard. However, the explosion in popularity of the Web was triggered by NCSA Mosaic which was a graphical browser running originally on Unix but soon ported to the Apple Macintosh and Microsoft Windows platforms. Version 1.0 was released in September 1993, and was dubbed the killer application of the Internet. Marc Andreessen, who was the leader of the Mosaic team at NCSA, quit to form a company that would later be known as Netscape Communications Corporation. Netscape released its flagship Navigator product in October 1994, and it took off the next year.

Microsoft, which had thus far not marketed a browser (in fact even as late as 1995 Bill Gates dismissed personal use of the World Wide Web as a passing fad), finally entered the fray with its Internet Explorer product, purchased from Spyglass, Inc. This began what is known as the browser wars, the fight for the Web browser market between Microsoft and Netscape.

The wars put the Web in the hands of millions of ordinary PC users, but showed how commercialization of the Web could stymie standards efforts. Both Microsoft and Netscape liberally incorporated proprietary extensions to HTML in their products, and tried to gain an edge by product differentiation, leading to the acceptance of the Cascading Style Sheets proposed by Håkon Wium Lie over Netscape's JavaScript Style Sheets (JSSS) by W3C.

In 1996, Netscape's share of the browser market reached 86% (with Internet Explorer edging up 10%); but then Microsoft began integrating its browser with its operating system and bundling deals with OEMs;, and within two years the trend had reversed. Although Microsoft has since faced antitrust litigation on these charges, the browser wars effectively ended once it was clear that Netscape's declining market share trend was irreversible.

In the second half of 2004 Internet Explorer had reached a peak market share of more than 92% . Ever since then, its market share had been slowly but steadily declining to less than 79% (May 2007).

Unable to continue commercially funding the product's development, Netscape responded by open sourcing its product, creating Mozilla. This helped the browser maintain its technical edge over Internet Explorer, but did nothing to slow Netscape's declining market share. The company was purchased by America Online in late 1998. At first, the Mozilla project struggled to attract developers, but by 2002 it had evolved into a relatively stable and powerful internet suite. Mozilla 1.0 was released to mark this milestone. Also in 2002, a spin off project that would eventually become the popular Mozilla Firefox was released. In 2004, Firefox 1.0 was released; Firefox 1.5 was released in November 2005. Firefox 2, a major update, was released in October 2006 and work has already begun on Firefox 3 which is scheduled for release in 2007. In 2006, Mozilla and its derivatives account for approximately 12% of Web traffic.

Opera, an innovative, speedy browser popular in handheld devices, particularly mobile phones, as well as on PCs in some countries was released in 1996 and remains a niche player in the PC Web browser market. It is available on Nintendo's DS, DS Lite and Wii consoles. The Opera Mini browser uses the Presto layout engine like all versions of Opera, but runs on most phones supporting Java Midlets.

The Lynx browser remains popular for Unix shell users and with vision impaired users due to its entirely text-based nature. There are also several text-mode browsers with advanced features, such as w3m, Links (which can operate both in text and graphical mode), and the Links forks such as ELinks.

Prior to the release of Mac OS X, Internet Explorer and Netscape were also the primary browsers in use on the Macintosh platform. However, Apple's Safari, the default browser on OS X from version 10.3 onwards, has since grown to dominate this market. Browsers such as Firefox and Camino are also popular amongst Mac users.

In 2003, Microsoft announced that Internet Explorer would no longer be made available as a separate product but would be part of the evolution of its Windows platform, and that no more releases for the Macintosh would be made. However, in early 2005, Microsoft changed its plans, announcing that version 7 of Internet Explorer was under development. IE 7 was released for Windows XP, Windows Server 2003, and Windows Vista in October 2006.

Types of Web Browsers

The following paragraphs discuss the properties of various web browsers.

WorldWideWeb

WorldWideWeb was the world's first Web browser and WYSIWYG HTML editor and was introduced on February 26, 1991 by Tim Berners-Lee and ran on the NeXTSTEP platform. It was later renamed Nexus to avoid confusion with the World Wide Web.

WorldWideWeb (WWW) was the first program which used not only the common File Transfer Protocol but also the Hypertext Transfer Protocol, invented by Berners-Lee in 1989. At the time it was written, WorldWideWeb was the only way to view the Web.

The source code was released into the public domain in 1993, thus making it free software.

A NeXT Computer was used by Berners-Lee as the world's first web server and also to write the first web browser, WorldWideWeb during the second half of 1990 while working for CERN. The first successful build was completed on Christmas Day, 1990, and successive builds circulated among Berners-Lee's colleagues at CERN before being released to the public (by way of Internet newsgroups) in August 1991. By this time, several others, including Bernd Pollermann, Robert Cailliau, Jean-François Groff, and graduate student Nicola Pellow (who wrote the line-mode browser), were involved in the project.

Berners-Lee and Groff later adapted many of WorldWideWeb's components into a C programming language version, creating the libwww API.

A number of early browsers appeared, notably ViolaWWW. They were all eclipsed by Mosaic in terms of popularity, which by 1993, had replaced the WorldWideWeb program. Those involved in its creation had moved on to other tasks, such as defining standards and guidelines for the further development of the World Wide Web-e.g. HTML, various communication protocols, and so on.

On April 30, 1993, the CERN directorate released the source code of WorldWideWeb into the public domain, making it free software. Several versions of the software are still available to download from evolt.org's browser archive. Berners-Lee initially considered releasing it under the GNU General Public License, but eventually opted for public domain to maximise corporate support.

Since WorldWideWeb was developed on and for the NeXTSTEP platform, the program used many of NeXTSTEP's components-WorldWideWeb's layout engine was built around NeXTSTEP's Text class.

WorldWideWeb was capable of displaying basic style sheets, downloading and opening any file type supported by the NeXT system (which included PostScript, movies, sounds, and so on), browsing newsgroups, and spellchecking. At first, images were displayed in separate windows, until NeXTSTEP's Text class supported Image objects.

The browser was also an editor. It allowed the simultaneous editing and linking of many pages in different windows. The functions "Mark Selection", which created an anchor, and "Link to Marked", which made the selected text an anchor linking to the last marked anchor, allowed the creation of links. Editing pages remotely was not yet possible, as the HTTP PUT method had not yet been implemented. Files would be edited in a local file system which was in turn served onto the web by an HTTP server.

WorldWideWeb's navigation panel contained Next and Previous buttons that would automatically navigate to the next or previous link on the last page visited, i.e., if one navigated to a page from a table of links, the Previous button would cause the browser to load the previous page linked in the table. This was useful for web pages which contained lists of links. Many still do, but the user interface metaphor was not adopted by other browser writers, and it disappeared. The same functionality is nowadays provided by publishers with explicit navigation buttons on web pages.

Erwise

Erwise was a popular web browser in the early days of the World Wide Web. At the time of its release in April 1992, one month prior to ViolaWWW, it was the world's first web browser with a graphical user interface for non-NeXT computers. The browser was written for Unix computers running X Window and used the W3 common access library. Erwise was a combined master's project of four Finnish students at the Helsinki University of Technology; Kim Nyberg, Teemu Rantanen, Kati Suominen and Kari Sydänmaanlakka. The group decided to create a web browser at the suggestion of Robert Cailliau, who was visiting the university. They were supervised by Ari Lemmke.

The development of Erwise froze after the students graduated and went on to other projects. Tim Berners-Lee, the creator of the World Wide Web, travelled to Finland to encourage the group to continue with the project. However, none of the project members could afford to continue with the project without proper funding. Berners-Lee couldn't continue their work either, as all the code was written in Finnish.

The name Erwise originates from otherwise and the name of the project group, OHT

ViolaWWW

ViolaWWW, first developed in the early 1990s, was the first popular web browser (though to a limited audience) which until Mosaic, was the most frequently used for access to the World Wide Web.

Gillies and Cailliau in How the Web was Born, offer an extensive history of the development of Viola. Viola was the invention of Pei-Yuan Wei, who at the time was a student at the University of California, Berkeley.

His interest in graphically based software began with HyperCard which he first discovered in 1989. Gillies and Cailliau quote Pei-Yuan Wei on this discovery: "HyperCard was very compelling back then, you know graphically, this hyperlink thing, it was just not very global and it only worked on Mac...and I didn't even have a Mac". Only having access to X terminals, he (in 1990) created the first version of Viola for them: "I got a HyperCard manual and looked at it and just basically took the concepts and implemented them in X-windows[sic]".

He released Viola 0.8 in 1991, and then after graduating began to develop Viola even further while working with "Berkeley's Experimental Computing Facility" as well as at a few start ups.

At this time, as Gillies and Cailliau indicate, Pei Wei's major goal was to create a version of Viola for the Internet:

> what Pei Wei wanted to do next was run it over the Internet. X-Window was a Unix-based system so it had TCP/IP built in and the Internet was a logical step. The question was how to transport his Viola pages across the Internet. He was on the verge of an independent invention of networked hypertext. 'And that's when I read Tim's e-mail about the World Wide Web' he explains 'The URL was very, very clever, it was perfectly what I needed. He dropped Tim a line saying that he was thinking of writing a browser for X. 'Sounds like a good idea,' said Tim in a reply posted to www-talk on 9 December. Four Days later, Pei Wei told www-talk that he had made a browser".

Created in 1992, it was the first browser to use authoring technology such as embedded scriptable objects, stylesheets, and tables. According to Gillies and Cailliau "Viola was to become the first X-browser to make any impact, but even his early versions went down well at CERN...As this ViolaWWW developed, it was to set the standard for everything to follow it...". Ed Kroll also highlighted it in his popular 1992 text, Whole Internet User's Guide and Catalog.

As ViolaWWW developed, it began to look more like HyperCard:

> It had a bookmark facility so that you could keep track of your favourite pages. It had buttons for going backwards and forwards and a history feature to keep track of the places you had been. As time went on, it acquired tables and graphics and by May 1993 it could even run programs.

It was based on the Viola toolkit, which is a tool for the development and support of visual interactive media applications, with a multimedia web browser being a possible application. Viola ran under the X Window System and could be used to build complex hypermedia applications that were beyond HTML 3.0 (the latest version of HTML at that time).

Viola was interesting because it was the first web browser to have the following features:

— client-side document insertion, predating frames which are used commonly today.

— a simple stylesheet mechanism used for inserting style information such as fonts, color and alignments into a document. This was implemented in Viola well before CSS was developed in 1998.

— a sidebar panel used for displaying "meta" information, intra document navigational links, and other information, similar to (but not as sophisticated as) features found in several modern browsers.

— a scripting language that can be accessed from an HTML document, such that an HTML document can embed highly interactive scripts/applets. This can be seen as the precursor to JavaScript and embedded objects.

While ViolaWWW opened the door to the World Wide Web, its limitations could not compete with Mosaic, the browser which brought the world wide web into the mainstream . According to Freedman in the Computer Desktop Encyclopedia, "Mosaic was 'the' application that caused interest in the World Wide Web to explode. Originally developed for UNIX, it was soon ported to Windows"

Because of ViolaWWW, Microsoft was allowed a retrial in February 2005 in the Microsoft v. Eolas case. The original ruling would have cost software giant Microsoft $521 million in damages. Eolas Technologies and the University of California sued Microsoft for allegedly infringing patents with the Internet Explorer web browser. The case revolved around a patent held by Eolas and the University which claims to cover ways of making other software work seamlessly with web browsers.

Microsoft had wanted to show the court ViolaWWW as prior art, since it was created in 1993 at the University of California, a year before the patent was filed. Microsoft had also suggested that Michael David Doyle, the founder of Eolas' and a former University of California researcher, had intentionally concealed his knowledge of ViolaWWW when filing the patent claim.

The Libwww Line Mode Browser

The first such browser was WWW - The Libwww Line Mode Browser, based on and shipped with the libwww library.

WWW - The Libwww Line Mode Browser was written before February 11, 1991 by Nicola Pellow, an intern working at CERN. The first stable version, 1.1 was released in January1992. Tim Berners-Lee had already written the first browser, WorldWideWeb, but that program only worked on NeXT computers, which were in limited use. So, Berners-Lee and his team recruited Pellow to write a browser so basic that it could run on any computer in existence at that time. The name "line-mode browser" is derived from that fact that, in order to ensure compatibility with the earliest computer terminals, such as Teletype machines, the program only displayed text one line at a time.

Mosaic

Mosaic was the first popular World Wide Web browser and Gopher client. It was reliable and easy to install, which opened the Web up to the general public. Mosaic was the first browser to actually implement images embedded in the text, rather than displayed in a separate window.

Mosaic was developed at the National Center for Supercomputing Applications (NCSA) beginning in late 1992. NCSA released the browser in 1993, and officially discontinued development and support on January 7, 1997. However, it can still be downloaded from NCSA.

Web browsers were the killer applications of the 1990s because they were the first programs to provide a multimedia graphical user interface to the Internet's burgeoning wealth of distributed information services (formerly limited to applications such as FTP, Usenet and Gopher). This was also a time when access to the Internet was expanding rapidly outside its previous domain of academia and large industrial research institutions.

Other browsers existed during this period, notably Erwise, ViolaWWW, Midas, and Cello. These browsers, however, would not create the same impact as Mosaic upon public use of the Internet. In the October 1994 Issue of Wired, Gary Wolfe notes in the article, "The (Second Phase of the) Revolution Has Begun: Don't look now, but Prodigy, AOL, and CompuServe are all suddenly obsolete - and Mosaic is well on its way to becoming the world's standard interface":

When it comes to smashing a paradigm, pleasure is not the most important thing. It is the only thing. If this sounds wrong, consider Mosaic. Mosaic is the celebrated graphical "browser" that allows users to travel through the world of electronic information using a point-and-click interface. Mosaic's charming appearance encourages users to load their own documents onto the Net, including color photos, sound bites, video clips, and hypertext "links" to other documents. By following the links - click, and the linked document appears - you can travel through the online world along paths of whim and intuition. Mosaic is not the most direct way to find online information. Nor is it the most powerful. It is merely the most pleasurable way, and in the 18 months since it was released, Mosaic has incited a rush of excitement and commercial energy unprecedented in the history of the Net.

Marc Andreessen and Eric Bina originally designed and programmed NCSA Mosaic for Unix's X Window System at NCSA. Funding for the development of Mosaic came from the High-Performance Computing and Communications Initiative, a programme created by the High Performance Computing and Communication Act of 1991 (or The Gore Bill after its author, then-Senator Al Gore).

Development of Mosaic began in December 1992. Version 1.0 was released on April 22, 1993, followed by two maintenance releases during summer 1993. A port of Mosaic to the Commodore Amiga was available by October 1993. Version 2.0 of NCSA Mosaic was released in December 1993, along with version 1.0 releases for both the Apple Macintosh and Microsoft Windows. An Acorn Archimedes port was underway in May 1994.

The licensing terms for NCSA Mosaic were generous for a proprietary software program. For all versions non-commercial use was generally free (with certain limitations). In addition the X Window System/Unix version publicly provided source code (source code for the other versions was available after agreements were signed). Despite persistent rumors to the contrary, however, Mosaic was never released as open source software during its brief reign as a major browser; there were always constraints on permissible uses without payment.

Marc Andreessen, the leader of the team that developed Mosaic, left NCSA and, with Jim Clark, one of the founders of Silicon Graphics, Inc. (SGI), and four other former students and staff of the University of Illinois, started Mosaic Communications Corporation. Mosaic Communications eventually became Netscape Communications Corporation, producing Netscape Navigator.

Spyglass licensed the technology and trademarks from NCSA for producing their own web browser but never used any of the NCSA Mosaic source code. Microsoft licensed Spyglass Mosaic in 1995 for US$2 million, modified it, and renamed it Internet Explorer. After a later auditing dispute, Microsoft paid Spyglass $8 million. The 1995 user guide The HTML Sourcebook: The Complete Guide to HTML, specifically states in a section called Coming Attractions, that Explorer "will be based on the Mosaic program" (p. 331). Versions of Internet Explorer before version 7 contained a credit to Spyglass and also NCSA Mosaic in the About box. Internet Explorer 7 was audited by Microsoft to ensure that it contained no Mosaic code, and thus no longer credits Spyglass or Mosaic.

Importance of Mosaic

Scholars consider Mosaic to be the web browser which led to the internet boom of the 1990s. Robert Reid underscores this importance stating, "while still an undergraduate, Marc wrote the Mosaic software...that made the web popularly relevant and touched off the revolution. It should be noted that Mosaic was not the first PC browser; this was Tom Bruce's little-known Cello. The UNIX version of Mosaic was already making it famous before the PC and Mac versions came out. Other than displaying images embedded in the text rather than in a separate window, Mosaic did not in fact add many features to the browsers it was modelled on, like ViolaWWW. But Mosaic was the first browser written and supported by a team of full-time programmers, which was reliable and easy enough for novices to install, and the inline graphics proved immensely appealing. Mosaic made the Web accessible to the ordinary person for the first time.

Reid also refers to Matthew Gray's well-respected website, Internet Statistics: Growth and Usage of the Web and the Internet, which indicates a dramatic leap in web use around the time of Mosaic's introduction

Marc Andreessen's realization of Mosaic, based on the work of Berners-Lee and the hypertext theorists before him, is generally recognized as the beginning of the web as it is now known. Mosaic, the first web browser to win over the Net masses, was released in 1993 and made freely accessible to the public. The adjective phenomenal, so often overused in this industry, is genuinely applicable to the...'explosion' in the growth of the web after Mosaic appeared on the scene. Starting with next to nothing, the rates of the web growth (quoted in the press) hovering around tens of thousands of percent over ridiculously short periods of time were no real surprise.;

Mosaic's popularity as a separate browser began to lessen upon the release of Andreessen's Netscape Navigator in 1994. As Ian S. Graham notes in the section called "Coming Attractions" in The HTML Sourcebook: The Complete Guide to HTML, "Netscape Communications has designed an all-new WWW browser Netscape, that has significant enhancements over the original Mosaic program".

By 1998 its userbase had almost completely evaporated. After NCSA stopped work on Mosaic, development of the NCSA Mosaic for the X Window System source code was continued by several independent groups. These independent development efforts include mMosaic (multicast Mosaic) which ceased development in early 2004 and VMS Mosaic which is under active development as of September 2007.

Netscape Navigator

Netscape Navigator, also known as Netscape, was a proprietary web browser that was popular during the 1990s. Once the flagship product of Netscape Communications Corporation and the dominant browser in usage share, its user base had almost completely evaporated by 2002, partly due to the inclusion of Microsoft's Internet Explorer web browser with the Windows operating system, but also due to lack of significant innovation after the late 1990s. Netscape's demise was a central component of Microsoft's antitrust trial, where the court ruled that (among other things) bundling Internet Explorer with Windows was an illegal monopolistic business practice.

The Navigator browser was succeeded by the Netscape Communicator internet suite, followed by later releases Netscape 6, Netscape 7 and Netscape Browser 8. However it was confirmed on 1 May 2007 the Netscape Navigator name would once again be re-generated in the next release of Netscape's browser, Netscape Navigator 9.

History and development

One of the central figures in the Netscape story is Marc Andreessen, cofounder of Netscape Communications Corporation and co-author of Mosaic at the National Center for Supercomputing Applications. After his graduation from Illinois in 1993, Andreessen moved to California to work at Enterprise Integration Technologies.

Andreessen then met with Jim Clark, the recently-departed founder of Silicon Graphics. Clark believed that the Mosaic browser had great commercial possibilities and provided the seed money. Soon Mosaic Communications Corporation was in business in Mountain View, California, with Andreessen appointed as a vice-president. The University of Illinois was unhappy with the company's use of the Mosaic name, so "Mosaic Communications Corporation" changed its name to Netscape Communications (thought up by sales representative Greg Sands) and its flagship web browser was the Netscape Navigator. Beta versions of the web browser were freely downloadable in mid- to late-1994, and version 1.0 of the browser was released by the end of the year.

The first few releases of the product were made available in "commercial" and "evaluation" versions; for example, version "1.0" and version "1.0N". The "N" evaluation versions were completely identical to the commercial versions; the letter was there to remind people to pay for the browser once they felt they had tried it long enough and were satisfied with it. This distinction was formally dropped within a year of the initial release, and the full version of the browser continued to be made available for free online, with boxed versions available on floppy disks (and later CDs) in stores along with a period of phone support. Email support was initially free, and remained so for a year or two until the volume of support requests grew too high.

During development, the Netscape browser was known by the code name Mozilla, which became the name of a Godzilla-like cartoon dragon mascot used prominently on the company's web site. Netscape was also the "killer" of Mosaic the other big browser at the time, Netscape therefore was called the Mosaic killer aka MoZilla. The Mozilla name was also used as the User-Agent in HTTP requests by the browser. Other web browsers claimed to be compatible with Netscape's extensions to HTML, and therefore used the same name in their User-Agent identifiers so that web servers would send them the same pages as were sent to Netscape browsers. A competitor's unauthorized use of a trademarked name could have been grounds for a lawsuit, but that possibility was left unexplored. Mozilla is now a generic name for matters related to the open source successor to Netscape Communicator.

Rise of Netscape

When the consumer Internet revolution arrived in the mid-to-late 1990s, Netscape was well positioned to take advantage of it. With a good mix of features and an attractive licensing scheme that allowed free use for non-commercial purposes, the Netscape browser soon became the de facto standard, particularly on the Windows platform. Internet service providers and computer magazine publishers helped make Navigator readily available.

An important innovation that Netscape introduced in 1994 was the on-the-fly display of webpages, where text and graphics appeared on the screen as the web page downloaded. Earlier web browsers would not display a page until all graphics on it had been loaded over the network connection; this made a user often have to stare at a blank page for as long as several minutes. With Netscape, people using dial-up connections could begin reading the text of a webpage within seconds of entering a web address, even before the rest of the text and graphics had finished downloading. This made the web much more tolerable to the average user.

Through the late 1990s, Netscape made sure that Navigator remained the technical leader among web browsers. Important new features included cookies, frames, and JavaScript (in version 2.0). Although those and other innovations eventually became open standards of the W3C and ECMA and were emulated by other browsers, they were often viewed as controversial. Netscape, according to critics, was more interested in bending the web to its own de facto "standards" (bypassing standards committees and thus marginalizing the commercial competition) than it was in fixing bugs in its products. Consumer rights advocates were particularly critical of cookies and of commercial web sites using them to invade individual privacy.

In the marketplace, however, these concerns made little difference. Netscape Navigator remained the market leader with more than 50% usage share. The browser software was available for a wide range of operating systems, including Windows (3.1, 95, 98, NT), Macintosh, Linux, OS/2, and many versions of Unix including DEC, Sun Solaris, BSDI, IRIX, AIX, and HP-UX, and looked and worked nearly identically on every one of them. Netscape began to experiment with prototypes of a web-based system, known internally as "Constellation", which would allow a user to access and edit his files anywhere across a network no matter what computer or operating system he happened to be using.

Industry observers confidently forecast the dawn of a new era of connected computing. The underlying operating system, it was believed, would become an unimportant consideration; future applications would run within a web browser. This was seen by Netscape as a clear opportunity to entrench Navigator at the heart of the next generation of computing, and thus gain the opportunity to expand into all manner of other software and service markets.

Fall of Netscape

Microsoft saw Netscape's success as a clear threat to the dominant status of the Microsoft Windows operating system. It began a wide-reaching campaign to establish control over the browser market. Browser market share, it was reasoned, leads to control over internet standards, and that in turn would provide the opportunity to sell software and services. Microsoft licensed the Mosaic source code from Spyglass, Inc., an offshoot of the University of Illinois, and turned it into Internet Explorer.

The resulting battle between the two companies became known as the browser wars. Versions 1.0 and 2.0 of IE were vastly inferior in almost every way to contemporary versions of Netscape Navigator; IE 3.0 (1996) began to catch up to its competition; IE 4.0 (1997) was the first version that looked to have Netscape beaten, and IE 5.0 (1998) with many bug fixes and stability improvements saw Navigator's marketshare plummet below IE for the first time.

Netscape Navigator 3.0 came in two versions, Standard Edition and Gold Edition. The latter consisted of the Navigator browser with mail and news readers and a web page WYSIWYG composition tool integrated into it. The extra functionality only made the software program larger, slower, and more prone to crashes, and the decision to integrate all these features together was widely criticized. But this integrated version became the only version when it was renamed Netscape Communicator in version 4.0; the product's name change (Netscape CEO Jim Barksdale insisted that Communicator was a general-purpose client application which contained the Navigator browser) diluted its name recognition and confused users.

The aging Communicator 4.x code could not keep up with Internet Explorer 5.0. Typical web pages had become graphics-heavy, often JavaScript-intensive, and were constructed with increasingly complex HTML code that used features designed for specific narrow purposes but redeployed them as global layout tools (in particular this applied to HTML tables, which Communicator struggled to render). The Netscape browser, once regarded as a reasonably solid product, came to be seen as crash-prone and buggy. It didn't help that some versions of it tended to re-download an entire web page to re-render it when the browser window was resized, a considerable nuisance to dial-up users, and would usually crash when the page contained anything but the most simple Cascading Style Sheets. In addition, the browser's somewhat dated-looking interface didn't have the modern appearance of Internet Explorer.

By the end of the decade, Netscape's web browser had unquestionably lost its former dominance on the Windows platform. Even on other platforms it was threatened, both by the gradual rise of open source browsers and by the August 1997 agreement that resulted in an investment of $150,000,000 by Microsoft in Apple, which included a requirement that Apple switch the default browser in new installations of Mac OS from Netscape to Internet Explorer. Of greatest significance, though, was Microsoft's massive and ultimately successful campaign to get ISPs and PC vendors to distribute Internet Explorer to their customers instead of Netscape. This was helped in part by Microsoft's investment in making IE brandable, such that it was a quick operation to create a customized version of IE. Also, web developers increasingly used proprietary, browser-specific extensions in the web pages they wrote. Both Microsoft and Netscape were guilty of this behavior, having added substantial proprietary HTML tags of their own into their browsers, the result of which was that users were forced to choose between two competing, almost entirely incompatible web browsers.

In March 1998, Netscape released most of the code base for Communicator under an open source license. The product named Netscape 5, which was intended to be the result, was never released, as managers decided that the poor quality of Netscape's code made a complete rewrite their only viable option. This product, taking growing contributions from the open-source community, was dubbed Mozilla, once the codename of the original Netscape Navigator. Netscape programmers gave Mozilla a different GUI and released it as Netscape 6 and later Netscape 7. After a lengthy public beta, Mozilla 1.0 was released on June 5, 2002. The same code base, most notably the Gecko layout engine, became the basis of several standalone applications, including Firefox and Thunderbird.

These products, however, suffered from a protracted development process that took several years to provide results, in the meantime America Online had bought out Netscape and released Netscape 6 off of a pre-beta quality build of the open source Mozilla browser, as a result, many users continued to migrate to Internet Explorer, and the Netscape browser itself has largely been abandoned.

Internet Explorer

Windows Internet Explorer (formerly Microsoft Internet Explorer abbreviated MSIE), commonly abbreviated to IE, is a series of proprietary graphical web browsers developed by Microsoft and included as part of the Microsoft Windows line of operating systems starting in 1995.

After the first release for Windows 95, additional versions of Internet Explorer were developed for other operating systems: Internet Explorer for Mac and Internet Explorer for UNIX (the latter for use through the X Window System on Solaris and HP-UX). Only the Windows version remains in active development; the Mac OS X version is no longer supported. It has been the most widely used web browser since 1999, peaking at nearly 90% market share with IE6 in the early 2000s-corresponding to over 900 million users worldwide by 2006.

Though released in 1995 as part of the initial OEM release of Windows 95, Internet Explorer was not included in the first retail, or shrink-wrap, release of Windows 95. The most recent release is version 7.0, which is available as a free update for Windows XP with Service Pack 2, and Windows Server 2003 with Service Pack 1 or later, and is included with Windows Vista. Versions of Internet Explorer prior to 6.0 SP2 are also available as a separate download for versions of Windows prior to Windows XP. An embedded OEM version called Internet Explorer for Windows CE (IE CE) is also available for WinCE based platforms and is currently based on IE6. Another Windows CE/ Windows Mobile browser known as Internet Explorer Mobile is from a different codebase and should not be confused with desktop versions of the browser.

History of Internet Explorer

Internet Explorer began conceptually as one of the major components of the unreleased Windows 97, imagined as the successor to Windows 95. The project was started in the summer of 1994 by Thomas Reardon and subsequently led by Benjamin Slivka, leveraging source code from Spyglass, Inc. Mosaic, an early commercial web browser with formal ties to the pioneering NCSA Mosaic browser. In late 1994, Microsoft licensed Spyglass Mosaic for a quarterly fee plus a percentage of Microsoft's non-

Windows revenues for the software. Although bearing a name similar to NCSA Mosaic, which was the first widely used web browser, Spyglass Mosaic was relatively unknown in its day and used the NCSA Mosaic source code only sparingly.

Versions 1, 2, and 3

Internet Explorer was not widely used until the release of version 3, which was the first version developed without Spyglass source code (although still using Spyglass "technology", so the Spyglass licensing information remained in the program's documentation). Internet Explorer 3 was the first major browser with CSS support, although this support was only partial. Released on August 13, 1996, it also introduced support for ActiveX controls, Java applets, inline multimedia, and the PICS system for content metadata. These were significant improvements compared to its main competitor at the time, Netscape Navigator. Version 3 also came bundled with Internet Mail and News, NetMeeting, and an early version of the Windows Address Book, and was itself included with Windows 95 OSR 2. Version 3 proved to be the first popular version of Internet Explorer, which brought with it increased scrutiny. In the months following its release, a number of security and privacy vulnerabilities were found by researchers and hackers.

Version 4

Version 4, released in September 1997, deepened the level of integration between the web browser and the underlying operating system. Installing version 4 on a Windows 95 or Windows NT 4 machine and choosing "Windows Desktop Update" would result in the traditional Windows Explorer being replaced by a version more akin to a web browser interface, as well as the Windows desktop itself being web-enabled via Active Desktop. The integration with Windows, however, was subject to numerous packaging criticisms. This option was no longer available with the installers for later versions of Internet Explorer but was not removed from the system if already installed. Internet Explorer 4 introduced support for Group Policy, allowing companies to configure and lock down many aspects of the browser's configuration. Internet Mail and News was replaced with Outlook Express, and Microsoft Chat and an improved NetMeeting were also included. This version also was included with Windows 98.

Version 5

Version 5, launched on March 18, 1999, and subsequently included with Windows 98 Second Edition and bundled with Office 2000, was another significant release that supported bi-directional text, ruby characters, XML, XSL and the ability to save web pages in MHTML format. (Windows 2000 included Internet Explorer 5.01 instead.)

Also, with the release of Internet Explorer 5.0, Microsoft released the first version of XMLHttpRequest, giving birth to Ajax (even though the term "Ajax" wasn't coined until years later.)

Version 5.5 followed in July 2000, improving its print preview capabilities, CSS and HTML standards support, and developer APIs; this version was bundled with Windows Me. Version 5.5 also included support for 128-bit encryption.

Version 6

Version 6 was released on August 27, 2001, a few weeks before Windows XP. This version included DHTML enhancements, content restricted inline frames, and partial support of CSS level 1, DOM level 1 and SMIL 2.0. The MSXML engine was also updated to version 3.0. Other new features included a new version of the Internet Explorer Administration Kit (IEAK), Media bar, Windows Messenger integration, fault collection, automatic image resizing, P3P, and a new look-and-feel that was in line with the "Luna" visual style of Windows XP. In 2002, the Gopher protocol was disabled and support for it was dropped in Internet Explorer 7.

Version 7

On February 15, 2005, Microsoft Chairman Bill Gates announced that the new version of its browser would be released at the RSA Conference 2005 in San Francisco. Internet Explorer 7 is available only for Windows XP SP2 and later, including Windows Server 2003 SP1 and Windows Vista. Sometime in October 2006, prior to the launch of IE7, Yahoo provided a post-beta version of Internet Explorer 7 bundled with a new version of Yahoo Messenger. The first beta version of the browser was released on July 27, 2005 for technical testing, and a first public preview version of Internet Explorer 7 (Beta 2 preview: Pre-Beta 2 version) was released on January 31, 2006. The final public version was released on October 18, 2006.

Version 7 is intended to defend users from phishing as well as deceptive or malicious software, and it also features full user control of ActiveX and better security framework, including not being integrated as much with Windows as previous versions, thereby increasing security. Unlike previous versions, the Internet Explorer ActiveX control is not hosted in the Windows Explorer process, but rather it runs in it own process. It also includes bug fixes, enhancements to its support for web standards, tabbed browsing with tab preview and management, a multiple-engine search box, a web feeds reader, Internationalized Domain Name support (IDN), and antiphishing filter.

Version 8

Version 8 of Internet Explorer is in development as written by Chris Wilson on the IEBlog. From the blog and based on the conferences of MIX 2007; RSS, CSS, AJAX, microformats, more options for user interface customization and improved web development tools are possibilities for inclusion into the forthcoming version of Internet Explorer, with security still being the top priority. Support for more of the CSS 2.1 specification as well as changes to the DOM for interoperability with other web browsers is in the cards.

Features

Internet Explorer has been designed to view the broadest range of web pages and to provide certain features within the operating system, including Microsoft Update. During the heyday of the historic browser wars, Internet Explorer superseded Netscape by supporting many of the progressive features of the time.

Component architecture

The Component Object Model (COM) technology is used extensively in Internet Explorer. It allows third parties to add functionality via Browser Helper Objects (BHO); and allows websites to offer rich content via ActiveX. As these objects can have the same privileges as the browser itself (in certain situations), there is a concern over security. Recent versions of Internet Explorer provide an Add-on Manager for controlling ActiveX controls and Browser Helper Objects and a "No Add-Ons" version (Under Programs/Accessories/System Tools).

Usability and accessibility

Internet Explorer makes use of the accessibility framework provided in Windows. Internet Explorer is also a user interface for FTP, with operations similar to that of Windows Explorer (although this feature requires a shell window to be opened in recent versions of the browser, rather than natively within the browser). Visual Basic for Applications (VBA) is not supported, but available via extension (iMacros).

Recent versions feature pop-up blocking and tabbed browsing. Tabbed browsing can also be added to older versions by installing Microsoft's MSN Search Toolbar.

Security framework

Internet Explorer uses a zone-based security framework, which means that sites are grouped based upon certain conditions. It allows the restriction of broad areas of functionality, and also allows specific functions to be restricted.

Patches and updates to the browser are released periodically and made available through the Windows Update service, as well as through Automatic Updates. Although security patches continue to be released for a range of platforms, most recent feature additions and security improvements are released for Windows XP only.

Recent versions of Internet Explorer provide Download Monitoring and Install Monitoring allowing users the choice of whether or not to download and install executables, in two stages. This helps to prevent installation of malware. Executable files downloaded using Internet Explorer are marked by the operating system as being potentially unsafe, and will prompt the user to confirm they want to run the executable every time, until the user confirms the file is "safe".

Group policy

Internet Explorer is fully configurable using Group Policy. Administrators of Windows Server domains can apply and enforce a variety of settings that affect the user interface (such as disabling menu items and individual configuration options), as well as underlying security features such as downloading of files, zone configuration, per-site settings, ActiveX control behavior, and others. Policy settings can be configured on a per-user and per-machine basis.

Standards support

Internet Explorer, using the Trident layout engine, almost fully supports HTML 4.01, CSS Level 1, XML 1.0 and DOM Level 1, with minor implementation gaps. It partially supports CSS Level 2 and DOM Level 2, with some implementation gaps and conformance issues. XML support brings with it support for XHTML, however Microsoft has buried this support since IE 5.0 making it difficult to access. Like other browsers it can consume XHTML when served as MIME type "text/html". It can also consume XHTML as XML when served as MIME types "application/xml" and "text/xml", however this requires a small XSLT measure to re-enable the XHTML as XML support. It pretends to not comprehend XHTML when vended in the preferred type as "application/xhtml+xml" and instead treats it as an unfamiliar file type for download.

Internet Explorer uses DOCTYPE sniffing to choose between "quirks mode" (renders similarly to older versions of MSIE) and standards mode (renders closer to W3C's specifications) for HTML and CSS rendering on screen (for printing Internet Explorer always uses standards mode). It fully supports XSLT 1.0 or the December 1998 Working Draft of XSL, depending on the version of MSXML (a dynamic link library) available. It also provides its own dialect of ECMAScript called JScript.

Opera

Opera is a cross-platform web browser and Internet suite which handles common Internet-related tasks including visiting web sites, sending and receiving e-mail messages, managing contacts, chatting online, viewing Widgets, downloading BitTorrents, and reading Newsfeeds. Opera's lightweight mobile web browser Opera Mini and most current versions of its desktop application are offered free of charge.

Opera is proprietary software developed by Opera Software based in Oslo, Norway. It runs on a variety of operating systems including many versions of Microsoft Windows, Mac OS X, Linux, FreeBSD and Solaris. It is also used in mobile phones, smartphones, Personal Digital Assistants, Nintendo DS, Wii and interactive televisions. Technology from Opera is also licensed by other companies for use in such products as Adobe Creative Suite.

Opera began in 1994 as a research project at Telenor, the largest Norwegian telecommunications company. In 1995 it branched out into an independent company named Opera Software ASA.

With version 2.0 the first public release was made in 1996. Due to popular demand version 3.0 was released for multiple operating systems in the end of 1997.

Opera version 5.0 became ad-sponsored instead of having a trial period. With version 8.5 the ad-banner was removed and the browser also stayed free of charge.

In version 9.1, Opera Software ASA introduced a fraud protection by Geotrust and Phishtank

Future developments

Opera 10 will be based on a cross-platform experience which will allow the user to begin reading a web page on the desktop, then continue on a mobile phone or PDA. Opera 10 will also include tools that will provide a platform for developers based on open standards. The future of Opera is lying on three different code bases, named "Merlin", "Kestrel", and "Peregrine".

Merlin. Merlin is the current code base used for version 9.0x, 9.1 and 9.2. It will see only minor feature improvements and mostly bugfixes. After 9.2 Merlin will no longer be used. Major improvements such as rendering improvements are not planned for the Merlin code base. A Merlin beta build with the new Speed Dial Browsing feature was released on February 28, 2007. In that same build Opera introduced support for animated GIFs in skins.

Kestrel. Kestrel is the code base closing the gap between Merlin and Peregrine, to be released as Opera 9.5. It will see some of the rendering improvements due to be made in Peregrine, and will also head to connect the Opera versions on different systems. As Peregrine builds are to be released in 2007, the first alpha Kestrel build was released on September 4, 2007.

Kestrel will support many more CSS3 selectors, the text-shadow property, and bug fixes to standards support. Kestrel's SVG implementation is improved, now supporting 93.4% of the SVG test suite. The interface will undergo a few minor alterations, one of which is adding back in screen reader support. Opera's mail client, M2, will be updated, sporting brand new backend and indexing, and also fixing some outstanding bugs. Kestrel will also have the ability of online synchronization of bookmarks, personal bar and Speed Dial settings using My Opera. Kestrel will also support APNG 1.0

Peregrine. Peregrine is the code base which will see the most improvements. It will have new features, new rendering improvements, bug fixes and perhaps a new GUI. First builds are to be released in 2007. Peregrine will likely be named Opera 10.

CSS3 support. David Storey, the chief Web opener at Opera Software, has announced that there will be improved CSS3 support in upcoming releases. A major focus will be on CSS3 selectors; this will allow authors to select HTML and XML elements more easily than they could using selectors from previous versions of CSS. For example, the last element in an element will be selectable via the CSS3 pseudo-class last-child, empty elements will be selectable via the CSS3 pseudo-class empty, and so forth. Additionally, there will be a new pseudo-class called nth-child, which will, for example, allow an author to dynamically define alternating background colors for HTML/XHTML list or table elements without having to resort to the use of scripting languages. Support for the CSS2/3 text-shadow property is also planned for Opera 9.5.

Features

In addition to the web browser, the other main component in the desktop versions of the Opera suite is the Opera Mail client, previously known as M2. Opera Mail supports regular POP and SMTP mail as well as IMAP. It also has an Address book. Opera Mail also features a newsreader and a newsfeed reader for RSS and Atom, as well as an IRC client for online chat.

Usability, accessibility. Opera was designed to run on low-end and small computers, with a commitment to computer accessibility for users who may have visual or mobility impairments. It also caters to a wide variety of personal preferences in the user interface as a multimodal browser.

— It is possible to control nearly every aspect of the browser using only the keyboard, and the default keyboard key definitions can be modified to suit the user. The product supplies several popular styles of key mappings; for example in one, the keys for editing a form entry are similar to those of Emacs. Opera also implements access keys, which allow a computer user to immediately jump to a specific part of a web page via the keyboard. Opera was also one of the first browsers to have mouse gestures, allowing patterns of mouse movement to trigger browser actions, such as "back" or "refresh".

— Page zooming allows text, images and other content such as Macromedia Flash, Java and Scalable Vector Graphics to be increased or decreased in size (20% to 1000%) to help those with impaired vision. User stylesheets may also be used to do this and to enable high contrast coloured fonts.

— Voice control, co-developed with IBM, allows control of the browser without the use of a keyboard or mouse. It can also read aloud pages and marked text. IBM has a browser based on Opera.

— A "Fit to Window" feature that relies on technology similar to Opera Mini's Small Screen Rendering (SSR), allowing websites to fit within a smaller screen without the need for horizontal scrolling.

Speed Dial Browsing. Opera 9.20 has "Speed Dial Browsing". The "Blank Page" when a new tab is opened is replaced with a page with nine slots which the user can set to contain a webpage. This feature is based on the speed dial browsing in Opera Mini.

Image Loading. Opera has long had the option to load a page without graphics, or to use only images in the cache. This was very useful when dial up via modem was the overwhelming method for using a web browser. It remains useful today with overloaded servers.

Download manager. Opera allows the user to list, pause, resume or restart the downloading of files. It also keeps history of recently downloaded files and allows opening them from within the browser. Opera 9 is also packaged with a torrent plugin, so BitTorrent downloads can be handled just like regular HTTP/FTP downloads. Opera can also be used with external download managers.

Extensions. Opera has been criticized for not providing an architecture to add application extensions to the browser, although it does support User JavaScript (including Greasemonkey scripts) and Widgets. Opera has supported User JavaScript extensions since version 8. Those scripts execute when pages are loaded and are used to enhance site functionality. UserJS.org is the unofficial central repository for Opera User JavaScripts. Userscripts.org lists scripts designed for the Greasemonkey Firefox extension, but many of them also work with Opera.

MDI and Tabs. Tabbed browsing with a true multiple document interface (MDI) was an original Opera innovation in the field of publicly available web browsers. This means multiple web pages can be opened within the same application window and resized, moved, tiled and cascaded like normal application windows in the operating system. Additional tab features include thumbnail previews for the page contained in each tab. Most modern browsers now offer tabbed browsing, but not all will use true MDI.

A feature of Opera's tabbed browsing is that Opera can be exited and restarted with all tabs and windows and their navigation histories still intact. Also, if a tab is closed accidentally its history has still been retained and the tab can be reopened using Undo(Ctrl-Z).

In subsequent years the default settings have changed from MDI to the simpler concept of tabs. Since version 6.0, Opera offers users the choice of three modes: Tabs, MDI, and SDI (No tabs).

Notes. This built-in tool allows the user to copy and paste content into a built-in text editor & archive. Clicking on the Note takes the user back to the web page from which it was originally copied.

Pop-up blocking. By default Opera blocks all unrequested pop up windows, but does allow the user to control their behavior in a variety of ways, such as forcing them into a background tab, or caching for later viewing. The user can also temporarily enable pop-ups for a specific site, or allow all pop-ups.

Privacy control. Opera can be configured to use proxy servers. It has an inbuilt cookie editor and cache viewer. Also, a powerful password managing tool called Wand is integrated into the browser.

Search facilities. Opera provides quick access to a variety of search engines and commerce sites, via the use of search plugins. Many search plugins are included with the browser, but they can also be user-defined or installed from an external sources. Opera also allows a user to translate a paragraph or look for meaning of a word directly by a right mouse click.

With the latest version of Opera, a user can have access to any search engine without opening the corresponding page. Right click in a search field and then use the "create search" option. The search engine will be listed in Opera in the future. Each search engine can have shortcut keyword. Typing in this shortcut keyword followed by space and search keyword into address field and going to that address will open page with search results of this search engine. Search engines that come with Opera by default have one character shortcut keywords.

Sessions. Opera allows the user to save a collection of open pages as a session, which can be opened later. Saved sessions include the independent histories and settings of each tab and window, including scroll positions, and could even be used to transfer an entire session to another computer.

Standards. Since version 3.5, Opera has supported CSS, and Håkon Wium Lie, one of the inventors of CSS, is the CTO at Opera. Up to 6.0 Opera supported most common web standards. Netscape plugins and some other recent standards such as WAP and WML for wireless devices, but its implementation of advanced ECMAScript (better known as "JavaScript") and the HTML Document Object Model was poor.

Version 7.0 saw Opera undergo an extensive rewrite with the older Elektra layout engine being replaced with the faster and more powerful Presto layout engine. The new engine brought almost full support for the HTML DOM meaning that parts of, or a whole, page can be re-rendered in response to DOM and script events. This release also saw incorporation into Adobe Dreamweaver, for the rendering of web graphics.

Version 8.0 introduced support for Scalable Vector Graphics (SVG) 1.1 Tiny. This marked the first major web browser to natively support some form of SVG. Opera has a presentation mode called Opera Show, which allows the use of a single HTML or XML document for large-screen presentations, and web browsing.

Version 9.0 is the first Microsoft Windows browser that passes the Acid2 test. This version adds XSLT and improves SVG to 1.1 Basic level.

Trash can. Opera has a "trash can" button, which allows the user to retrieve blocked pop-ups or a tab closed earlier in the same session. The list of deleted tabs is kept until the session is closed, and can be used as a temporary bookmark during the session.

User defined themes. Opera supports customized user interfaces themes, allowing users to change the location and style of toolbars, buttons and menus. A drag and drop functionality allows the user to easily place links and buttons on toolbars. Many user-created themes, ranging from color changes to OS adaptations can be downloaded and installed with a few clicks thanks to the built-in automatic installer.

7

Search Engines

A search engine is an information retrieval system designed to help find information stored on a computer system. Search engines help to minimize the time required to find information and the amount of information which must be consulted, akin to other techniques for managing information overload. The most popular form of a search engine is a Web search engine which searches for information on the public World Wide Web. Other kinds of search engines include enterprise search engines, which search on intranets, personal search engines, and mobile search engines.

Functioning of a Search Engines

Querying

Search engines provide an interface to a group of items that enables users to specify criteria about an item of interest and have the engine find the matching items within the group. In the most popular form of search, items are documents or web pages and the criteria are words or concepts that the documents may contain.

There are several varieties of syntax in which a search engine user can express a query. Some methods are formalized and require a strict, logical and algebraic syntax. Other approaches are less strict and allow for a less defined query. One form of a less-restricted query syntax is referred to as Natural Language Search, which is a term typically used to describe web search engines that apply natural language processing of some form.

For example, instead of searching for one or two words, a query could consist of an English sentence or paragraph. A natural language search engine will then parse the query into words and evaluate searches for these words. This places less burden on the search engine user to formulate a specific query using restrictive, and sometimes difficult to learn, syntax. A second definition of natural language search engines reflects how the search engine performs indexing, unrelated to the query syntax. This requires a semantic understanding of the query in order to disambiguate the text.

Traditional search engines tend to use a non-linguistic model of language and the hypothesis is that NLS will provide better results - that is to say, results that more accurately and efficiently support a user's need.

Ranking

A Boolean search for an item within a group of items will either return the exact matching item or nothing. This is a rather orthodox search method where the equality between the desired item and the actual item must be exact. In application, it is sometimes far more beneficial and useful to incorporate a more lax measure of similarity between the desired item(s) and the items that exist in the group being searched. For example, instead of finding only the exact book in a library, a library search engine may return a list of 'similar' books, with the exact book listed first.

The list of items that meet the criteria specified by the query are typically sorted, or ranked, in some regard so as to place the most 'relevant' items first. Placing the most relevant items first reduces the time required by users to determine whether one or more of the resulting items are sufficiently similar to the query. It has become common knowledge through the use of Web search engines that the further down the list of matching items you browse, the less relevant the items become.

Indexing

To provide a set of matching items quickly, a search engine will typically collect information, or metadata, about the group of items under consideration beforehand. For example, a library search engine may determine the author of each book automatically and add the author name to a description of each book.

Users can then search for books by the author's name. Other metadata in this example might include the book title, the number of pages in the book, the date it was published, and so forth. The metadata collected about each item is typically stored on a computer in the form of an index. The index typically requires a smaller amount of computer storage and provides a way for the search engine to calculate the relevance, or similarity, between the query and the set of items.

Helpful Features

Users can save time in typing correct words with auto correct options enable/disable. Highlighter such as yellow line markers help in highlighting certain search item on the results. Could be used for copying and editing as well.

Predictive search engines such as study consumer or end user pattern in presenting results. Variants of search engines present personalized data. Web search engines provide an interface to search for information on the World

Wide Web. Information may consist of web pages, images and other types of files. Some search engines also mine data available in newsgroups, databases, or open directories. Unlike Web directories, which are maintained by human editors, search engines operate algorithmically or are a mixture of algorithmic and human input.

History of Web Search Engines

The very first tool used for searching on the Internet was Archie. The name stands for "archive" without the "v". It was created in 1990 by Alan Emtage, a student at McGill University in Montreal. The program downloaded the directory listings of all the files located on public anonymous FTP (File Transfer Protocol) sites, creating a searchable database of file names; however, Archie did not index the contents of these files.

The rise of Gopher (created in 1991 by Mark McCahill at the University of Minnesota) led to two new search programs, Veronica and Jughead. Like Archie, they searched the file names and titles stored in Gopher index systems. Veronica (Very Easy Rodent-Oriented Net-wide Index to Computerized Archives) provided a keyword search of most Gopher menu titles in the entire Gopher listings. Jughead (Jonzy's Universal Gopher Hierarchy Excavation And Display) was a tool for obtaining menu information from specific Gopher servers. While the name of the search engine "Archie" was not a reference to the Archie comic book series, "Veronica" and "Jughead" are characters in the series, thus referencing their predecessor.

The first Web search engine was Wandex, a now-defunct index collected by the World Wide Web Wanderer, a web crawler developed by Matthew Gray at MIT in 1993. Another very early search engine, Aliweb, also appeared in 1993, and still runs today. JumpStation (released in early

1994) used a crawler to find web pages for searching, but search was limited to the title of web pages only. One of the first "full text" crawler-based search engine was WebCrawler, which came out in 1994.

Unlike its predecessors, it let users search for any word in any webpage, which became the standard for all major search engines since. It was also the first one to be widely known by the public. Also in 1994 Lycos (which started at Carnegie Mellon University) was launched, and became a major commercial endeavor.

Soon after, many search engines appeared and vied for popularity. These included Excite, Infoseek, Inktomi, Northern Light, and AltaVista. In some ways, they competed with popular directories such as Yahoo!. Later, the directories integrated or added on search engine technology for greater functionality.

Search engines were also known as some of the brightest stars in the Internet investing frenzy that occurred in the late 1990s. Several companies entered the market spectacularly, receiving record gains during their initial public offerings. Some have taken down their public search engine, and are marketing enterprise-only editions, such as Northern Light.

Google

Around 2001, the Google search engine rose to prominence. Its success was based in part on the concept of link popularity and PageRank. The number of other websites and webpages that link to a given page is taken into consideration with PageRank, on the premise that good or desirable pages are linked to more than others. The PageRank of linking pages and the number of links on these pages contribute to the PageRank of the linked page. This makes it possible for Google to order its results by how many websites link to each found page. Google's minimalist user interface is very popular with users, and has since spawned a number of imitators.

Google and most other web engines utilize not only PageRank but more than 150 criteria to determine relevancy. The algorithm "remembers" where it has been and indexes the number of cross-links and relates these into groupings. PageRank is based on citation analysis that was developed in the 1950s by Eugene Garfield at the University of Pennsylvania.

Google's founders cite Garfield's work in their original paper. In this way virtual communities of webpages are found. Teoma's search technology uses a communities approach in its ranking algorithm. NEC Research Institute has worked on similar technology. Web link analysis was first developed by Jon Kleinberg and his team while working on the CLEVER project at IBM's Almaden Research Center. Google is currently the most popular search engine.

Yahoo! Search

The two founders of Yahoo!, David Filo and Jerry Yang, Ph.D. candidates in Electrical Engineering at Stanford University, started their guide in a campus trailer in February 1994 as a way to keep track of their personal interests on the Internet. Before long they were spending more time on their home-brewed lists of favourite links than on their doctoral dissertations. Eventually, Jerry and David's lists became too long and unwieldy, and they broke them out into categories. When the categories became too full, they developed subcategories ... and the core concept behind Yahoo! was born.

In 2002, Yahoo! acquired Inktomi and in 2003, Yahoo! acquired Overture, which owned AlltheWeb and AltaVista.

Despite owning its own search engine, Yahoo! initially kept using Google to provide its users with search results on its main website Yahoo.com. However, in 2004, Yahoo! launched its own search engine based on the combined technologies of its acquisitions and providing a service that gave pre-eminence to the Web search engine over the directory.

Microsoft

The most recent major search engine is MSN Search (evolved into Live Search), owned by Microsoft, which previously relied on others for its search engine listings. In 2004, it debuted a beta version of its own results, powered by its own web crawler (called msnbot). In early 2005 , it started showing its own results live, and ceased using results from Inktomi, now owned by Yahoo!. In 2006, Microsoft migrated to a new search platform - Live Search, retiring the "MSN Search" name in the process.

Baidu

Due to the difference between hanzi and the Roman alphabet, the Chinese search market did not boom until the introduction of Baidu in 2000.

Challenges Faced by Search Engines

The Web is growing much faster than any present-technology search engine can possibly index see distributed web crawling. In 2006, some users found major search-engines became slower to index new webpages. Many webpages are updated frequently, which forces the search engine to revisit them periodically.

The Web search queries one can make are currently limited to searching for key words, which may result in many Type I and type II errors positives, especially using the default whole-page search. Better results might be achieved by using a Proximity search (text) option with a search-bracket to limit matches within a paragraph or phrase, rather than matching random words scattered across large pages. Another alternative is using human operators to do the researching for the user with organic search engines.

Dynamically generated sites may be slow or difficult to index, or may result in excessive results, perhaps generating 500 times more webpages than average. Example: for a dynamic webpage which changes content based on entries inserted from a database, a search-engine might be requested to index 50,000 static webpages for 50,000 different parameter values passed to that dynamic webpage. The indexing is numerous in the dynamic webpages, they can also be shown by logical thinking: if one parameter-value generates 1 indexed webpage, 10 generate 10, and 1,000 parameter-values generate 1,000 webpages, etc.

Many dynamically generated websites are not indexable by search engines; this phenomenon is known as the invisible web. There are list of search engines that specialize in crawling the invisible web by crawling sites that have dynamic content, require forms to be filled out, or are password protected.

Some search-engines do not rank results by relevance, but by the amount of money the matching websites pay. In 2006, hundreds of generated websites used tricks to manipulate a search-engine to display them in the higher results for numerous keywords. This can lead to some search engine results being polluted with linkspam or bait-and-switch pages which contain little or no information about the matching phrases. The more relevant webpages are pushed further down in the results list, perhaps by

500 entries or more. For example, many spammers create websites containing random sequences of high-traffic keywords, often with misspellings in order to attract a higher ranking on a search engine.

Secure pages content hosted on HTTPS URLs pose a challenge for crawlers which either can't browse the content for technical reasons or won't index it for privacy reasons.

Web search engines work by storing information about a large number of web pages, which they retrieve from the WWW itself. These pages are retrieved by a Web crawler (sometimes also known as a spider) - an automated Web browser which follows every link it sees. Exclusions can be made by the use of robots.txt. The contents of each page are then analyzed to determine how it should be indexed (for example, words are extracted from the titles, headings, or special fields called meta tags).

Data about web pages are stored in an index database for use in later queries. Some search engines, such as Google, store all or part of the source page (referred to as a cache) as well as information about the web pages, whereas others, such as AltaVista, store every word of every page they find. This cached page always holds the actual search text since it is the one that was actually indexed, so it can be very useful when the content of the current page has been updated and the search terms are no longer in it.

This problem might be considered to be a mild form of linkrot, and Google's handling of it increases usability by satisfying user expectations that the search terms will be on the returned webpage. This satisfies the principle of least astonishment since the user normally expects the search terms to be on the returned pages. Increased search relevance makes these cached pages very useful, even beyond the fact that they may contain data that may no longer be available elsewhere.

When a user enters a query into a search engine (typically by using key words), the engine examines its index and provides a listing of best-matching web pages according to its criteria, usually with a short summary containing the document's title and sometimes parts of the text. Most search engines support the use of the boolean operators AND, OR and NOT to further specify the search query. Some search engines provide an advanced feature called proximity search which allows users to define the distance between keywords.

The usefulness of a search engine depends on the relevance of the result set it gives back. While there may be millions of webpages that include a particular word or phrase, some pages may be more relevant, popular, or authoritative than others.

Most search engines employ methods to rank the results to provide the "best" results first. How a search engine decides which pages are the best matches, and what order the results should be shown in, varies widely from one engine to another. The methods also change over time as Internet usage changes and new techniques evolve.

Most Web search engines are commercial ventures supported by advertising revenue and, as a result, some employ the controversial practice of allowing advertisers to pay money to have their listings ranked higher in search results. Those search engines which do not accept money for their search engine results make money by running search related ads alongside the regular search engine results.

The search engines make money every time someone clicks on one of these ads.The vast majority of search engines are run by private companies using proprietary algorithms and closed databases, though some are open source.

Storage Costs and Crawling Time

Storage costs are not the limiting resource in search engine implementation. Simply storing 10 billion pages of 10 kbytes each (compressed) requires 100TB and another 100 TB or so for indexes, giving a total hardware cost of under $200k: 100 cheap PCs each with four 500GB disk drives. However, a public search engine requires considerably more resources than this to calculate query results and to provide high availability.

Also, the costs of operating a large server farm are not trivial. Crawling 10B pages with 100 machines crawling at 100 pages/second would take 1M seconds, or 11.6 days on a very high capacity Internet connection. Most search engines crawl a small fraction of the Web (10-20% pages) at around this frequency or better, but also crawl dynamic websites (e.g. news sites and blogs) at a much higher frequency.

Geospatially-enabled Web Search Engines

A recent enhancement to search engine technology is the addition of geocoding and geoparsing to the processing of the ingested documents being indexed, to enable searching within a specified locality (or region). Geoparsing attempts to match any found references to locations and places to a geospatial frame of reference, such as a street address, gazetteer locations, or to an area (such as a polygonal boundary for a municipality). Through this geoparsing process, latitudes and longitudes are assigned to the found places, and these latitudes and longitudes are indexed for later spatial query and retrieval.

This can enhance the search process tremendously by allowing a user to search for documents within a given map extent, or conversely, plot the location of documents matching a given keyword to analyze incidence and clustering, or any combination of the two.

Social Search

A social search engine is a type of search engine that determines the relevance of search results by considering the interactions or contributions of users. Example forms of user input include social bookmarking or direct interaction with the search results such as promoting or demoting results the user feels are more or less relevant to their query.

When applied to Web search this user-based approach to relevance is in contrast to established algorithmic or machine-based approaches where relevance is determined by analyzing the text of each document or the link structure of the documents (ex: the basis of PageRank). Social search takes many forms, ranging from simple shared bookmarks or tagging of content with descriptive labels to more sophisticated approaches that combine human intelligence with computer algorithms.

Social search began to emerge between 2004 and 2005. On January 21, 2004 Eurekster was referred to as personalized social search . On June 28, 2005 Jeremy Zawodny at Yahoo referred to the Yahoo! MyWeb product as 'social search'. On October 26, 2005 Pete Cashmore applied the term 'social search' to Wink.

And despite the current awareness, the concept of social search can be considered to derive from Google's PageRank algorithm, which assigns importance to Web pages based on analysis of the link structure of the web, because PageRank is relying on the collective judgement of webmasters linking to other content on the web. Links, in essence, are positive votes by the webmaster community for their favorite sites.

Social search as it's evolving today incorporates both automated software as well as human judgments about the nature of web content.

Social search is information retrieval, wayfinding tools informed by human judgment. It's about people helping people find stuff. Social search experiences revolve around the outcome of collaborative harvesting, directory building, tagging, social ranking, Question & Answers services, Shared bookmarks and Web pages. Social Search is surfacing the tail and already channeling significant amounts of traffic around. Information retrieval is reaching another inflexion point.

There is a shift taking place from Search engines having the power to search users getting empowered, from the head to the tail, from a "few-to-many" to a "many-to-many" publishing model. Social search is changing the rules, shifting power to the people. Another way to think of it is Social Search is the 3rd big evolution of the search business after:

i) algorithmic search,

ii) paid search models, and now

iii) Social Search.

Web 2.0 trends converge toward social search: social networking, consumer generated media, open platforms and syndication models, new user interaction models. To paraphrase Microsoft's Ramez Naam, it's like every human being is a neuron, and humanity as a whole is one giant brain, smarter as a connected whole. If you can increase the ability of humans to communicate with each other, you make the whole planet smarter.

As articulated by Chris Sherman, social search is information retrieval, way finding tools informed by human judgment. Social search is people helping people find stuff using plain-language questions and answers, collaborative content harvesting, directory building, voting and ranking, sharing, tagging, commenting on bookmarks, Web pages, news, images, videos and podcasts.

Benefits

To date social search engines have not demonstrated measureably improved search results over algorithmic search engines. However, there are potential benefits deriving from the human input qualities of social search.

— Reduced impact of Link Spam by relying less on link structure of Web pages

— Increased relevance because each result has been selected by users

— Leverage a network of trusted individuals by providing an indication of whether they thought a particular result was good or bad

— The introduction of 'human judgement' suggests that each Web page has been viewed and endorsed by one or more people, and they have concluded it is relevant and worthy of being shared with others using human techniques that go beyond the computer's current ability to analyze a Web page.

— Web pages are considered to be relevant from the reader's perspective, rather than the author who desires their content to be viewed, or the Web master as they create links.

— More current results. Because a social search engine is constantly getting feedback it is potentially able to display results that are more current or in context with changing information

Because users can directly add results to a social search engine there is a risk that some users could insert Search Spam directly into the search engine. Elimination or prevention of this spam would require the ability to detect the validity of a users' contribution, such as whether it agrees with other trusted users.

The Long Tail of search is a concept that there are so many unique searches conducted that most searches, while valid, are performed very infrequently. A search engine that relied on users filling in all the searches would be at a disadvantage to one that used machines to crawl and index the entire Web.

Vertical Search

Vertical search, part of a larger subgrouping known as "specialized" search, is a relatively new tier in the Internet search industry consisting of search engines that focus on specific businesses. While Google, Yahoo!, and the like will continue to dominate the online consumer search market, research analysts say many specialized search engines are emerging to address the particular information needs of niche audiences and professions.

Niche search engines are not new. Web sites that help users find people, shop and get business information have existed for years. But the number of these search engines being introduced has greatly increased in recent years.

In fact, in the last three years, research analysts at Forrester Research, Jupiter Research and MarketingSherpa have identified a new tier in search dubbed "specialized search", which includes "local", "topical" and "vertical" search. Local search is already a burgeoning subset, with

Google Local and many newspapers offering this functionality.

Like consumers, businesses use the Internet for a variety of needs. Sometimes they're looking for all the information they can get, and for that the likes of Google and the Yahoo search engines are used. But more often they're looking for something very specific related to their businesses. That's where vertical search sites come in. Vertical search engines deliver to businesses what the big sites can't without the use of complex keyword combinations: relevant and essential content versus an exhaustive return of information.

Vertical Search vs. Broad-based Search

To see how these sites differ, it's helpful to know how they are designed. The term "search engine" refers to a software program that searches the Web and Usenet groups to find documents for a specified keyword and returns a list of documents in which the keyword was found.

Broad-based search engines such as Google or Yahoo fetch very large numbers of documents using a Web crawler. Another program called an indexer then reads these documents and creates a search index based on words contained in each document. Each search engine uses a proprietary algorithm to create its indexes so that, ideally, only meaningful results are returned for each query.

Vertical search engines, on the other hand, send their spiders out to a highly refined database, and their indexes contain information about a specific topic. As a result, they are of most value to people interested in a particular area; what's more, the companies that advertise on these search engines reach a very focused audience. For example, there are search engines for veterinarians, doctors, patients, job seekers, house hunters, recruiters, travelers and corporate purchasers, to name a few.

Vertical Search User

As the broad-based search engines have gotten broader, so have their search results. This has become increasingly frustrating to users who have turned to search engines to find information on a specialized topic, be it local information, travel sites or specific business channels.

This is especially true of the latter. In the business marketing profession, terms that have very specific meanings in certain industries will yield a host of irrelevant results when used as keywords on the big search engines.

For example, say a dentist is looking for information on ceramics, a common material used in dental work. If the dentist performs a Google search on the keyword "ceramics", Google will serve up millions of results, but most of the entries on the first few pages will concern hobbies like pottery. On the other hand, if the dentist performs the same search on DentalProducts.net, a well-regarded media company Web site, it will return much more relevant results.

LookSmart, an online media and technology company that has launched more than 180 vertical search sites, contends that Web users will increasingly use the Internet the way they do cable television, opting for specialized channels that speak directly to their concerns. This company says vertical search engines will chip away at Google's and Yahoo's audiences the same way cable TV channels such as TLC and the National Geographic Channel have eaten into network audiences.

Buyer in Vertical Search Marketing

On the simplest level, the vertical search buyer is a marketer that wants to be found by the user of one of these specialized search engines. When a business person searches the Web through a search engine or a directory, that person is considered to be in "hunt mode". Marketers understand that this hunt mode means the searcher may very well be somewhere in the buying cycle. That makes search engine results some of the best sources of targeted traffic, whether that traffic originates from "organic" unpaid search listings or paid advertising listings. "Vertical search providers will play an important role in the paid search market in the next five years," said Zia Wigder, vice president and research director at JupiterResearch, a division of JupiterMedia. "Search marketers must establish a robust management strategy and an efficient testing and inclusion process to profit from this growth."

Growth in Vertical Search

Advertisers on vertical sites are able to reach potential customers who are much closer to making a purchase decision than the average user on Google or Yahoo, according to Greg Sterling, an analyst with The Kelsey Group. He told Forbes.com that that's the whole motivation for advertising on vertical sites. For example, he said someone doing a search on Edmunds.com, an automobile search engine, is probably more serious about buying a car than someone doing a car search on a general search engine.

The cost of advertising on the large search engines is also likely to drive more marketers to vertical search.

"Increasing competition and rising keyword prices should motivate search marketers to look for newer, viable opportunities to diversify their incoming traffic", said Sapna Satagopan, research associate at JupiterResearch.

"Vertical search is about to happen", says Gary Stein, director of strategy at Ammo Marketing and a former senior analyst at JupiterMedia. "Market conditions are setting up for it: the popularity of search engines; the availability of tools to build it; and opportunities to make money-advertisers are competing for keywords."

A study by JupiterResearch called "Vertical Search: Early Marketers Will Reap Rewards of Low Pricing" found that paid search is densely concentrated within primary categories, or verticals: retail, financial services, travel, and media and entertainment. These accounted for 79% of spending on paid search in the United States in 2004.

Vertical Search Design and Advertising Models

In terms of design and implementation, several models are emerging in vertical search:

— The vertical search engine as a destination or portal. Often media companies that own these destination sites optimize them and buy keywords on Google to drive their audience to visit.

— Vertical search as a complementary Web site application: This model entails embedding a search engine box on an existing, already trafficked site. One example is CertMag.com.

— Parametric search: This tool, more prevalent in engineering and other product-specific, information-intensive, procurement-driven industries, often allows for face-to-face product and manufacturer comparison.

In terms of revenue that these vertical search engines generate, a variety of advertising programs are gaining favor, including:

— Cost per click, in which the advertiser pays only for each time that a user clicks on its ad.

— Cost per thousand/cost per impression/cost per view, the standardized, traditional method of online advertising, is now emerging as an option in vertical search environments.

— Cost per action, an emerging model in which the advertiser pays, not on click, or for impressions, but only if the consumer performs a specific action, such as purchases a good.

— Flat fee/fixed fee, the most popular early ad model for most of the vertical search engines.

— Web order entry/self-service, a system whereby marketers can buy, monitor and revise their ad campaigns themselves simply by entering their credit card information through a password-protected interface.

— Paid inclusion, the practice of inserting "editorial-like" ads or more traditional ads into the actual organic search results.

— Paid listing, in which ads appear on top of or beside organic listings and are clearly identified as sponsored links.

— Free, plus, in which the site is completely free for both those listing and those searching, with additional features available for those who pay.

Metasearch Engine

A meta-search engine is a search engine that sends user requests to several other search engines and/or databases and returns the results from each one. Meta search enables users to enter search criteria once and access several search engines simultaneously. Since it is hard to catalogue the entire web, the idea is that by searching multiple search engines you are able to search more of the web in less time and do it with only one click. The ease of use and high probability of finding the desired page(s) make metasearch engines popular with those who are willing to weed through the lists of irrelevant 'matches'. Another use is to get at least some results when no result had been obtained with traditional search engines.

Metasearch engines create what is known as a virtual database. They do not compile a physical database or catalogue of the web. Instead, they take a user's request, pass it to several other heterogeneous databases and then compile the results in a homogeneous manner based on a specific algorithm.

No two metasearch engines are alike. Some search only the most popular search engines while others also search lesser-known engines, newsgroups, and other databases. They also differ in how the results are presented and the quantity of engines that are used. Some will list results according to search engine or database. Others return results according to relevance, often concealing which search engine returned which results. This benefits the user by eliminating duplicate hits and grouping the most relevant ones at the top of the list.

Search engines frequently have different ways they expect requests submitted. For example, some search engines allow the usage of the word "AND" while others require "+" and others require only a space to combine words. The better metasearch engines try to synthesize requests appropriately when submitting them.

Results can vary between metasearch engines based on a large number of variables. Still, even the most basic metasearch engine will allow more of the web to be searched at once than any one stand-alone search engine. On the other hand, the results are said to be less relevant, since a metasearch engine can't know the internal "alchemy" a search engine does on its result (a metasearch engine do not have any direct access to the search engines' database).

Search Engine Marketing

Search Engine Marketing, or SEM, is a form of Internet Marketing that seeks to promote websites by increasing their visibility in the Search Engine results pages (SERPs). According to the Search Engine Marketing Professionals Organization, SEM methods include: Search Engine Optimization (or SEO), paid placement, and paid inclusion. Other sources, including the New York Times, define SEM as the practice of buying paid search listings with the goal of obtaining better free search listings.

In 2006, North American advertisers spent US$9.4 billion on search engine marketing, a 62% increase over the prior year and a 750% increase over the 2002 year. The largest SEM vendors are Google AdWords, Yahoo! Search Marketing and Microsoft adCenter. As of 2006, SEM was growing much faster than traditional advertising.

As the number of sites on the Web increased in the mid-to-late 90s, search engines started appearing to help people find information quickly. Search engines developed business models to finance their services, such as pay per click programs offered by Open Text in 1996 and then Goto.com in 1998. Goto.com later changed its name to Overture in 2001, and was purchased by Yahoo! in 2003, and now offers paid search opportunities for advertisers through Yahoo! Search Marketing. Google also began to offer advertisements on search results pages in 2000 through the Google AdWords program. By 2007 pay-per-click programs proved to be primary money-makers for search engines.

Search Engine Optimization consultants expanded their offerings to help businesses learn about and use the advertising opportunites offered by search engines, and new agencies focusing primarily upon marketing and advertising through search engines emerged. The term "Search Engine Marketing" was proposed by Danny Sullivan in 2001 to cover the spectrum of activities involved in performing SEO, managing paid listings at the search engines, submitting sites to directories, and developing online marketing strategies for businesses, organizations, and individuals. In 2007 Search Engine Marketing is Stronger than ever with SEM Budgets up 750% as shown with stats dating back to 2002 vs 2006.

Paid search advertising hasn't been without controversy, and issues around how many search engines present advertising on their pages of search result sets have been the target of a series of studies and reports by Consumer Reports WebWatch, from Consumers Union. The FTC also issued a letter in 2002 about the importance of disclosure of paid advertising on search engines, in response to a complaint from Commercial Alert, a consumer advocacy group with ties to Ralph Nader.

Desktop Search

Desktop search is the name for the field of search tools which search the contents of a user's own computer files, rather than searching the Internet. These tools are designed to find information on the user's PC, including web browser histories, e-mail archives, text documents, sound files, images and video.

One of the main advantages of desktop search programs is that search results come up in a few seconds, much faster than was possible with previous tools such as Windows XP's search companions.

Desktop search is emerging as a concern for large firms for two main reasons: untapped productivity and security. A commonly cited statistic states that 80% of a company's data is locked up inside unstructured data - the information stored on an end user's PC, the files and directories they've created on a network, documents stored in repositories such as corporate intranets and a multitude of other locations. Moreover, many companies have structured or unstructured information stored in older file formats to which they don't have ready access.

Companies doing business in the United States are frequently required under regulatory mandates like Sarbanes-Oxley, HIPAA and FERPA to make sure that access to sensitive information is 100% controlled. This creates a challenge for IT organizations, which may not have a desktop search standard, or lack strict central control over end users downloading tools from the Internet. Some consumer-oriented desktop search tools make it possible to generate indexes outside the corporate firewall and share those indexes with unauthorized users. In some cases, end users are able to index - but not preview - items they should not even know exist.

Technologies

Desktop search engines build and maintain an index database to achieve reasonable performance when searching several gigabytes of data. Indexing usually takes place when the computer is idle and most search applications can be set to suspend it if a portable computer is running on batteries, in order to save power. When indexing the files, desktop search tools collect three types of information about files:

— file and directory names

— metadata, such as titles, authors, comments in file types such as MP3, PDF and JPEG

— content of supported documents.

To search within documents, the tools need to be able to parse many different types of documents. This is achieved by using filters that interpret selected file formats. For example, a Microsoft Office Filter might be used to search inside Microsoft Office documents.

Long-term goals for desktop search include the ability to search the contents of image files, sound files and video by context .

The sector has attracted considerable attention from the emerging struggle between Microsoft and Google. According to market analysts, both companies are attempting to leverage their monopolies (of web browsers and search engines, respectively) to strengthen their dominance. This may bring back memories of the browser wars of the 1990's.

Mobile Search

Mobile Search is an evolving branch of information retrieval services that is centered around the convergence of search engines and mobile phones or other mobile devices. The services allow users to find content that is being specifically written for, or adapted for, mobile devices as well as search the web through a mobile device optimized interface.

Competition for the US mobile search market promises to be fierce, thanks to the large US online ad market and strong pushes by portals. By 2011, mobile search will account for around $715 million, or almost 15% of a total mobile advertising market worth nearly $4.7 billion", according to a leading market research firm. Depending on a researcher's particular bias toward telecom, Web or technology factors, the published forecasts for global mobile search vary from $1.5 billion by 2011 (from Informa Telecoms & Media) to over $11 billion by 2008 (according to Piper Jaffray).

Mobile Search is important for the usability of mobile content for the same reasons as internet search engines became important to the usability of internet content. Early internet content was largely provided by portals such as Netscape. As the depth of available content grew, portals were unable to provide total coverage. As a result internet search engines such as Google and AltaVista proved popular as a way of allowing users to find the increasingly specialist content they were looking for.

There is a similar situation developing in the mobile content industry. Given early adopter usage of mobile services, there has been a vast increase in the depth of content developed for mobile phones. There are now few large organizations that do not offer a mobile service of some sort. Most of the operators run their own portals that showcase the best available content. However, given the limitations of a mobile phones screen size and general navigability, most of available content that has been written for mobile users is effectively invisible to users. Research from Qpass suggests that less than 36% of an operator's portal is within 30 seconds navigation distance for the user - this being the expected time users expect to find content in.

The early deals are taking place as cellphone operators recognize that mobile Internet search is an inherently different business than its desktop counterpart. Whereas people might use a Web-connected personal computer to search for information about an 18th-century British author, they are more likely to use cellphones to find targeted information like news, weather and sports. Cellphones also offer much less space to enter in search terms and smaller screens to display results.

Some of the advancements by the major portals in Internet search, such as Google's famous page-ranking scheme, don't apply in the mobile world since people aren't searching for Web sites as much as answers to specific questions. Alltel's group president of operations, Kevin Beebe, says the Internet search giants aren't yet delivering the kind of results the mobile content industry wants. "What they're trying to do is take that core search capability and just jam it onto the phone," Mr. Beebe said. "That's probably not the right approach."

"Mobile search is a battle to define perhaps the most important new interface with the consumer," says John du Pre Gauntt, eMarketer Senior Analyst and the author of the new report, Mobile Search: Clash of the Titans. "Whoever cracks the consumer and commercial code for delivering and monetizing relevant answers for people on the go will secure a license to print money, at least for a time."

Mobile Search Services

Within the broad umbrella of Mobile Search (the ability to browse for mobile specific content), there are a range of services. Given the relative immaturity of the market, not all of these can be expected to become the industry standards.

Mobile Optimized Search Engines - Most major search engines have implemented a mobile optimized version of their products that take into consideration bandwidth and form factor limitations of the mobile platform. For example, Yahoo has launched a product branded as Yahoo OneSearch and Google has launched a mobile friendly version of their search engine as well.

Mobile question and answer services - These services allow a user to text a question to a central database and receive a reply using text. A usage example would be a user that wants to know the answer to a very specific question but is not in front of his/her computer. Most mobile 'Q&A' services are powered by human researchers. A new approach by AskMeNow is to use Semantic Web technology to automate the process.

Mobile Directory Search - This service is known by different names dependent on country and operator. It can also be known as 'Find My Nearest' or 'Mobile Yellow Pages' services. The basics of the services allows users to find local services in the vicinity of their current location. The services often use location-based technology to pinpoint exactly where the user currently is.

An example of usage would be a user looking for a local cab or taxi company after a night out. Services also usually come with a map and directions to help the user. An example is the service offered by Yell in the UK which is powered by MobilePeople's technology. More details can be found in mobile local search.

Mobile Discovery Services. These services offer users recommendations on what they should do next. An example would be recommending a user a similar ringtone to the one that s/he has just browsed for. They operate, in a mobile context, in a similar way to the recommendation engines provided by internet retail shops such as Amazon.com.

An example of real usage is the Directory Enquiries (DQ) service operated by Orange in the UK. Callers to the Orange landline DQ service are given the business and residential numbers they have requested verbally by an operator. In addition, Orange sends the information in text format to the users mobile phone. The information contains a text reminder of the requested information as well as links to local businesses, services and other interesting information in the local area that the user has searched on.

Mobile Navigation Services. These services provide the indexing structure to the portals provided by mobile operators. They index the content already on the Operators' portal but also provide users access to mobile specific content that is available outside the confines of the portal.

General Search Engines

Google

Google is owned by Google, Inc. whose mission statement is to "organize the world's information and make it universally accessible and useful". The largest search engine on the web, Google receives several hundred million queries each day through its various services.

PageRank

Google uses an algorithm called PageRank to rank web pages that match a given search string. The PageRank algorithm computes a recursive figure of merit for web pages, based on the weighted sum of the PageRanks of the pages linking to them. The PageRank thus derives from human-generated links, and correlates well with human concepts of importance.

Previous keyword-based methods of ranking search results, used by many search engines that were once more popular than Google, would rank pages by how often the search terms occurred in the page, or how strongly associated the search terms were within each resulting page. In addition to PageRank, Google also uses other secret criteria for determining the ranking of pages on result lists.

Search results

Google not only indexes and caches HTML files but also 13 other file types, which include PDF, Word documents, Excel spreadsheets, Flash SWF, plain text files, among others. Except in the case of text and SWF files, the cached version is a conversion to HTML, allowing those without the corresponding viewer application to read the file.

Users can customize the search engine somewhat. They can set a default language, use "SafeSearch" filtering technology (which is on 'moderate' setting by default), and set the number of results shown on each page. Google has been criticized for placing long-term cookies on users' machines to store these preferences, a tactic which also enables them to track a user's search terms over time. For any query (of which only the 32 first keywords are taken into account), up to the first 1000 results can be shown with a maximum of 100 displayed per page.

Advanced search operators

Google's searches are not limited to reporting back indexed pages corresponding to the search query. A variety of advanced search operators can be used to perform more sophisticated queries.

Non-Web sources of data

Despite its immense index, there is also a considerable amount of data in databases, which are accessible from websites by means of queries, but not by links. This so-called deep web is minimally covered by Google and contains, for example, catalogs of libraries, official legislative documents of governments, phone books, and more.

Google optimization

Since Google is the most popular search engine, many

webmasters have become eager to influence their website's Google rankings. An industry of consultants has arisen to help websites raise their rankings on Google and on other search engines. This field, called search engine optimization, attempts to discern patterns in search engine listings, and then develop a methodology for improving rankings.

As Google's algorithms and results have gained the trust of web users, commercial websites will profit from subverting these results by artificially inflating their rankings. Some search engine optimization firms have attempted to inflate specific Google rankings by various artifices, and thereby draw more searchers to their client's sites. One of Google's main challenges has been to weaken some of these attempts by reducing the ranking of sites known to use them.

Search engine optimization encompasses both "on page" factors (like body copy, title tags, H1 heading tags and image alt attributes) and "Off Page Optimisation" factors (like anchor text and PageRank). The general idea is to affect Google's relevance algorithm by incorporating the keywords being targeted in various places "on page", in particular the title tag and the body copy. Too many occurrences of the keyword, however, cause the page to look suspect to Google's spam checking algorithms.

One "Off Page Optimisation" technique that works particularly well is Google selling in which websites link to another site using a particular phrase in the anchor text, in order to give the site a high ranking when the word is searched for.

The Google webmaster guidelines were published for website owners who would like to raise their rankings when using legitimate optimization consultants.

Uses of Google

A corollary use of Google - and other Internet search engines - is that it can help translators to determine the most common way of expressing ideas in the English language (and other languages). This is generally done by doing a 'count' of different variants, thereby establishing which expression is more common. While this approach requires careful judgement, it does improve the ability of non-native translators to use more idiomatically correct English expressions.

Google dance

Google dance refers to the period of time when Google indexes are tuned. This will often cause both a fluctuation in index size as well a significant change in a web site's search result position.

Search engine features

Besides the main search engine feature of searching for text, the search engine can be used as a calculator, currency converter, dictionary and many others as well.

Search products

In addition to its tool for searching webpages, Google also provides services for searching images, Usenet newsgroups, news websites, videos, searching by locality, maps, and items for sale online. In 2006, Google has indexed over 25 billion web pages, 1.3 billion images, and over one billion Usenet messages. It also caches much of the content that it indexes. Google operates other tools and services including Google News, Google Suggest, Froogle, Google Maps, Google Co-op and Google Desktop Search.

There are also products available from Google that are not directly search-related. Gmail, for example, is a webmail application, but still include search features;

Google Browser Sync does not offer any search facilities, although it aims to organise your browsing time.

Yahoo! Search

Yahoo! Search is a web search engine, owned by Yahoo!. Originally, "Yahoo! Search" merely referred to a Yahoo! provided interface, which would send queries to another search engine "behind the scenes". The results were presented to the user under the Yahoo! brand. Originally, none of the actual web crawling and storage/retrieval of data was done by Yahoo! itself.

Seeking to provide its own search engine results, Yahoo! acquired other companies with their own search engines. In 2002, it bought Inktomi, a "behind the scenes" search engine, whose results are shown on other companies' web sites.

In 2003, it bought Overture Services, Inc., which owned the AlltheWeb and AltaVista search engines. Initially, even though it owned multiple search engines, it didn't use them on the main Yahoo.com web site, but kept using Google's search engine for its results.

However, starting in 2003, Yahoo! Search became an original web crawler-based search engine, with a reinvented crawler called Yahoo! Slurp. Yahoo! Search combined the capabilities of search engine companies it had acquired, with its existing research, and put them into a single search engine.

Its new search engine results were included in all of Yahoo!'s sites that had a web search function. It also started to sell its search engine results to other companies, to show on their web sites. Its relationship with Google was terminated at that time, with the former partners becoming each other's main competitors.

AltaVista

The name AltaVista refers both to an Internet search engine company and to that company's search engine product.AltaVista was started by Digital Equipment Corporation employee volunteers who were trying to provide services to make finding files on the public network easier.

At launch the service had two innovations that set it ahead of the other search engines. It used a fast multi-threaded crawler (Scooter) that could cover a lot more Web pages than were believed to exist, and an efficient search back-end running on advanced hardware; as of 1998, 20 multi-processor machines using DEC's then-new Alpha processor, along with 130GB RAM and 500GB hard disk space each, receiving 13 million queries per day. These made AltaVista the first searchable, full-text database of a large part of the World Wide Web.

In 1996, AltaVista became the exclusive provider of search results for Yahoo!. In 1998, Digital was sold to Compaq, and in 1999 Compaq relaunched AltaVista as a web portal, abandoning their streamlined searchpage and alienating their core userbase. In June of the same year, Compaq paid AltaVista Technology Incorporated ("ATI") US$ 3.3 million for the domain name altavista.com, but it continued to lose marketshare, especially to Google. It was subsequently floated from Compaq as an independent company.

In February 2003, AltaVista was bought by Overture Services, Inc. The failed attempt at a "portal" was dropped and the website was again revamped to provide simple search functions. In October 2003, Overture itself was taken over by Yahoo!. In Aug. 2004, shortly after Yahoo!'s acquisition, the AltaVista site started using the Yahoo! Search database.

AltaVista was also one of the numerous websites which promised "free email for life", only to subsequently reverse this policy by charging a subscription fee for its email services.In 2001 it announced it would launch an ISP in the UK with no phone call charges and only a £10 a year subscription fee. However the service never launched.

AltaVista provides free translation, branded Babel Fish, which translates text between several world languages. AltaVista also has an "Adult Categories" feature in the video search, wich sort out types of pornogaphy such as Hardcore, Mature, and Blonde. This is much more accepting of the adult entertainment industry than competetors like google.

Ask.com

Ask.com, is an Internet search engine. It is also the company name of the division of IAC Search & Media, founded in 1996 by Garrett Gruener and David Warthen in Berkeley, California. The original software was implemented by Gary Chevsky from his own design. Three venture capital firms, Highland Capital, Institutional Venture Partners, and The RODA Group were early investors.

Ask.com was originally known as Ask Jeeves, where "Jeeves" is the name of the "gentleman's personal gentleman", or valet (illustrated by Marcos Sorenson), fetching answers to any question asked. The character was based on Jeeves, Bertie Wooster's fictional valet from the works of P. G. Wodehouse.

The original idea behind Ask Jeeves was to allow users to get answers to questions posed in everyday, natural language. Ask.com was the first commercial question-answering search engine for the World Wide

Web. It supports a variety of user queries in plain English (natural language), as well as traditional keyword searching and strives to be more intuitive and user-friendly than other search engines.

In other words, when you ask a question, it searches for the answer. Ask Jeeves sold the same technology used on the ask.com site to corporations including Dell, Toshiba, and E*Trade. That part of the business was sold to Kanisa in 2002.

As time passed and keyword search engines such as Google rose to prominence by indexing more webpages, Ask Jeeves suffered a loss of many of its users. The technology was reworked to allow keyword searches as well, but by this time Ask Jeeves had dropped below Google, MSN, and Yahoo! in the size of their userbase.

However, because Ask.com was slow to index some new webpages, Ask.com did not suffer the onslaught of computer-generated linkspam results that initially flooded Google Search, MSN Search, and Yahoo! Search and buried significant webpages that Ask Jeeves (or Ask.com) could still find.

Ask Jeeves, Inc. stock traded on the NASDAQ stock exchange from July 1999 to July 2005, under the ticker symbol ASKJ. At the time of the IPO in 1999, ASKJ had the 3rd best first-day performance in history. In 2003, it was the 51st best performing stock out of 3229 companies on the NASDAQ. The price of Ask Jeeves stock soared more than 500% throughout the course of the year. In July 2005, the ASKJ ticker was retired upon the closing of the acquisition by IAC/InterActiveCorp. IAC/InterActiveCorp trades on the NASDAQ under the ticker symbol IACI. The IAC/InterActiveCorp deal was announced in March 2005 valuing ASKJ at $1.85 billion. IAC/InterActiveCorp is a media holding company founded and run by Barry Diller.

Live Search

Live Search is the name of Microsoft's web search engine, successor to MSN Search, designed to compete with the industry leaders Google and Yahoo!. Live Search is accessible through Microsoft's Live.com and MSN web portal. The new search engine offers some innovative features, such as the ability to view additional search results on the same web page (instead of needing to click through to subsequent search result pages) and the ability to dynamically adjust the amount of information displayed for each search-result. It also allows the user to save searches and see them updated automatically on Live.com.

The first public beta of Live Search was unveiled on March 8, 2006, with the final release on September 11, 2006 replacing MSN Search. On March 21, 2007, it was announced that Microsoft would separate its Live Search developments from the Windows Live services family. Live Search was integrated into the Live Search and Ad Platform headed by Satya Nadella, part of Microsoft's Platform and Systems division. As part of this change, Live Search was consolidated with Microsoft adCenter.In the roll-over from MSN Search to Live Search, Microsoft stopped using Picsearch as their image search provider and started performing their own image search, fueled by their own internal image search algorithms.

Live Search Mobile allow search results to be displayed onto a mobile device. Live Product Upload and Live Search Books Publisher Program allow users to upload and publish their own contents to the search index and allow merchants and book publishers to search for them via Live Product Search and Live Search Books respectively.Microsoft also develops and operates other search tools and services including Windows Desktop Search.There are also many Windows Live services available that are not directly search-related. Windows

Live Hotmail, for example, is a webmail application, but still include search features.

Live Search Gadget is for Windows Vista's Sidebar that uses Live Search to fetch the user's search results and render them directly in the gadget. The gadget allow users to configure up to two additional custom searches. Users can also search using Live Search Macros from this gadget by creating their own macros or find one in Windows Live Gallery.

Live Search Traffic Gadget displays real-time traffic conditions using Live Search Maps. The gadget provides shortcuts to driving directions, local search and full-screen traffic view. Currently only traffic data from 23 selected US cities are supported, including Atlanta, Boston, Chicago, Denver, Detroit, Houston, Los Angeles, Milwaukee, New York, Oklahoma City, Philadelphia, Phoenix, Pittsburgh, Portland, Providence, Sacramento, Salt Lake City, San Diego, San Francisco, Seattle, St. Louis, Tampa, and Washington DC.

8

Educational Applications of Web

Nothing before has captured more the imagination and interest of educators simultaneously around the globe as has the World Wide Web. The Web, as we'll call it, is causing teachers, from pre-school to graduate school, to re-think the very nature of teaching, learning, and schooling. With the Web, teaching and learning can be freed from the boundaries of classrooms and class schedules. Traditional lectures and teacher presentations can become multimedia learning experiences for students. Learning resources of the school can be augmented by learning resources of the world via the Web. Moreover, the Web can help us re-focus our institutions from teaching to learning, from teacher to student.

Technological change, which not only permits new activities but makes those new activities superior in many important ways over the previous method of operation, creates long lasting innovations in society. Web-based education is one of those innovations. Why is the remarkably fast growing innovation of web-based education important to our world? Firstly, it is radically growing in the first world nations of the world, especially in the United States. This alone means that it will likely grow in other nations in the world, as this innovation dominates education at all levels. Secondly, teachers at all levels can merely post their syllabi on Blackboard but some have radically changed their whole method of teaching so that the class venue for the teacher and the student becomes the computer. The classroom now is a "virtual learning environment." Learning is no longer bound by space and time. To use a metaphor associated with the past, the traditional classroom has become the expensive and difficult to handle as the rolled parchment manuscript whenthe printing press innovation was implemented. Web-based education has become the cheaper and superior printed book of the modern era.

Web-based education means the most extreme form of online education that uses streaming videos and the more advanced functionalities available in educational software and where there is no actual face to face contact between the teacher and the student.

Functionalities of Web-based Education

There are seven important functionalities in web-based education:

(1) real time announcements,

(2) posting of text, html, spreadsheets, videos, PowerPoint, audio files,

(3) real time grade book,

(4) external links,

(5) discussion board and chat rooms,

(6) automated quizzes, and

(7) emails to individuals and list serves.

For the student, the announcements are on the opening page of the course. The announcements allow the teacher to give the students needed information items, as the course evolves during the semester. The student can view all the announcements or only the most recent as he or she wishes. This is very useful as the announcements are available immediately to the student as the teacher makes the posting. In addition, the teacher has a record of when the announcement was posted and modified. This leaves the student without the traditional classroom argument that "I did not hear the announcement."Most new users of online or web-based education use the announcements and the functionality of posting materials. Teachers find that posting their one or more page syllabus useful because the students have it easily available and can print it when they wish or as often as they wish. However, few teachers really take advantage of this functionality. For example, very few post their PowerPoint lecture notes or their lectures on Blackboard.

For beginners, the real time grade book, external links, and email functions are wonderful. Students want their grades posted as soon after the test as possible. With software like Blackboard, they can go to their grade book and see the instructor's grades as soon as they are posted. The added advantage is the software protects the privacy of the student by permitting the student to only see his or her grades. External links provide the student with Internet sources that are particularly important and useful from the teacher's point of view. The email function is very handy as it allows the teacher and student to easily communicate with each other or with the whole class as a group using a list-serve. In addition, there is a drop box capacity, which allows the student and teacher to send files and easily keep track of what was sent and when. This is especially useful for students submitting assignments or faculty returning assignments with their comments. For the more advanced users, the teacher can use automated quizzes. If the test is objective or uses "fill in the blank" but not subjective questions, the teacher can post the quizzes on the Internet and have the computer grade it automatically. The student goes to the quiz, enters the password for the quiz, and takes either a timed or non-timed quiz.

When finished and submitted, the computer tells the students which answers were incorrect, provides teacher feedback on each question, and enters the score in the gradebook. The teacher has the option of allowing the student to retake the exam or not. If security is a concern, the teacher can ask the students to take the online quiz in a controlled computer lab environment in which IDs would be checked and students would not have access to any other materials. The professor can also configure quizzes to have the computer randomly selects questions from a large question pool, which also helps discourage cheating.

For even more advanced professors using Blackboard, there is the discussion board / chat rooms. This permits students to interact with the teacher and other students with the computer. Chat rooms require students and the teacher to get on the computer at the same time and then communicate with each other over the computer screen. For those who wish student and instructor interactions, most users prefer the asynchronous discussion board, which is active for a set period of time such as a week. During that time, the teachers and students log-on and record their thoughts on the topic plus the comments of those who spoke earlier. All thoughts are captured on the computer. The advantage of the discussion board beyond the recording of comments is the opportunity given to the students of developing more thoughtful comments over a longer period of time. The activity of the teacher in a given discussion board forum can vary from nothing to strong guidance to keep the students on point and focus their comments.

The most advanced professors can also use software produced by Tegrity, Real Player, Apple's Final Cut, or Microsoft Producer. With this software, professors can record their lectures and post them on Blackboard using streaming video. All of these products allow professors to merge their PowerPoint lecture slides with a video of them lecturing using the slides. The functional advantages and prices of these various productsvary significantly. For example, Microsoft Producer requires a three step operation of preparing PowerPoint slides, capturing the video of the lecture, and integrating the slides with the video. The big advantage of Microsoft Producer is the zero cost for those who own PowerPoint 2002 or higher. In addition, professors can use other off the shelf software to prepare and then post audio and movie files using streaming video. If the professor posts a combination of video and audio lecture files, students can download the video files at the university high speed computers and the corresponding audio files at home using their phone line connection in seconds. However, if the students download videos from phone line connections, the normal download time for streaming video is much slower and the downloaded video quality is much less. Therefore, the professor is wise to post both video and audio only files of their lectures to maximize the students' ability to review the lectures with minimum frustration.

In these learning systems, the range of functionalities is not just an impressive array of IT bells and whistles. They have been designed with specific pedagogical and cognitive development theories supporting them. Given this range of functionalities, how can a teacher maximize the use of this software? Frankly, the answer varies according to the creative teaching style of the teacher. The approach presented here assumes an entire online experience and almost no face to face interaction with the teacher or other students. With this approach, students must learn how to operate in a "virtual" environment and thus the teacher must make sure the students have adequate training time in a computer lab. This training is essentially only for students taking their first online class.The more advanced users of web-based education should integrate the functionalities of Blackboard based on the teacher's course objective and the teacher's judgment on how to best present the material to the students.

First, the teacher needs to place on the web site all course material including syllabus, external links, reading materials except the required books, lectures, full instructions on all aspects of the class, quizzes / tests, videos and audio files, and so on.

Secondly, the teacher must consider how to us the quizzes to maximize the learning experience. For example, the teacher can use the quizzes, which the students take, to reinforce the text assignments and lectures. The teacher does this by merely allowing the student to retake those quizzes, which are then called "friendly" quizzes. In addition, the teacher should award a small portion of the total grade for these friendly quizzes in order to insure the students take them. Students will take the friendly quizzes, review the questions and correct answers carefully, and then retake them to improve their grade. The result for the teacher is that the computer takes attendance automatically and the computer re-enforces the key points of the lesson.

Another web-based teaching ploy involves teaching practical lessons such as analytical techniques. The teacher first presents the analytical concept with text and video lectures. Next, the teacher provides practice friendly quizzes so that the students can perform using the analytical technique correctly. Finally, the teacher provides nonfriendly quizzes on the technique to insure the students have actually learned the technique. In showing the technique, the teacher might wish to link the quizzes with spreadsheets or other software to make sure the student uses the technique with available software tools.

Thirdly, the teacher should consider how to use the discussion board to maximize the learning experience by reinforcing the text assignments and lectures using in-depth dialogue among the students. For example, the teacher can select six topics that can benefit from group interaction and thought. The teacher places the forum topics on the discussion board and might even break down each topic into sub-topics called "threads." The instructor then assigns students to small groups of six and defines three revolving roles during the semester. Four students are discussants, who must address the topic and threads on the forum discussion board for a period of one week. One student is a reporter, who must summarize the forum at the end of the week.

Finally, one student is the leader, who must get the students involved, promote active participation, and finally recommend for all other students in the group a forum grade to the instructor following the posted guidelines of the teacher. Based on the experience of one of the authors with discussion boards, the results vary from 20 to 90 comments that range from a few words to a several paragraphs.

The quality of the web-based discussion is much better than normal classroom discussion because the students have an opportunity to present more thoughtful comments. In web-based discussions over a period of one week, introverted students tend to be more active for several reasons. Any speech or social handicap is not apparent and feelings of inadequacy are less likely to inhibit their performance. They have more time to develop their thoughts, adjust them in the context of what is being said, correct them, and then submit them at their pace of thought. They do not have to compete emotionally with extroverts, who tend to dominate the relatively short classroom time.Students do the normal mid-term, final, and term paper. At least, the mid-term and possibly the final should be a comprehensive take home tests that requires integrative thought and should be submitted via the "drop box." Students should also submit the term paper via the drop box. An alternative and very challenging assignment to the term paper is to require students to prepare a Microsoft Producer file with PowerPoint and integrated video. An advantage of this approach is that the student learns a valuable new computer skill.

One problem with term papers is that students sometimes cheat by paying someone else to write their paper and catching this type of cheating is almost impossible. Another advantage of students preparing a Producer file is that their cheating is made more difficult because they must appear in the Producer file videos. Unfortunately, student cheating can occur in other ways in both traditional and web-based education. For example, if the teacher uses take home exams, students can merely pay other students to do the course work. To almost insure that cheating does not occur on a test, the teacher can use a cumulative objective final examination that the students must take in a secure computer lab, use a password given just for the test, and have the computer draw the final questions randomly from a large pool of questions. In web-based courses, students can easily pay another person to take their quizzes, tests, and term paper. Having at least one major class product done in a secure setting tends to discourage that form of cheating, as the teacher can easily require a pass in the secured test in order to pass the course.

IMPLICATIONS OF WEB-BASED EDUCATION

The implications of web-based education are staggering but they are particularly important to public administration education with its many part-time practitioner students. Regardless of the country, most beginning and even upper level public administrators are not properly trained in public administration. Yet, they are typically promoted from a professional expertise, in which they are competent, to one in which they have no or little training or education. Somehow, they must now be managers and need a completely different set of skills and knowledge from when they were engineers, accountants, or teachers.

These same people are typically remarkably busy and find going to graduate school very challenging in terms of the time commitment that requires them to balance heavy work load and school assignments with family obligations. Going 15 weeks to graduate school twice a week for a semester is more than a challenge to someone that lives a two hours commute to the nearest university offering the MPA degree, has a forty hour plus work week, and has family needs to fulfill. Thus, the needed education just does not happen or happens at the sacrifice of the job or family. Web-based education means that time and place are no longer barriers. Any student who can get to a computer can take a web-based class and get an education at least equal to the one offered at a traditional MPA program. In the United States and the other first world countries of the world, the limitation of computer access is not a major problem as they exist at the work place, in public libraries, and often in the homes of the students. The only serious computer problem that does exist is called "the last mile." This means that most computers are connected to the Internet using phone lines that have limited bandwidth, which results in a slow download time from the web. For the next decade, the solution for the professor is merely to post large files with video, such as Microsoft Producer files, to the web in two versions. One posting is with high quality video. The other posting is with an audio only option. Then the professor lets the student decide which option is most suitable for them when calling up those files.

In others countries, computer barriers are more significant. For example, free access in libraries does not exist in many places and students are not as likely to have computers at home. As in first world countries, bandwidth is also a serious handicap because the student will not be able to download large video files through telephone lines.

Unlike first world countries, bandwidth can also be a problem because the key route connectors are insufficiently narrow.In addition in some countries, customers are charged for Internet access by the size of the download files. This practice greatly discourages the use of multi-media over the Internet. Only infrastructure investment, time, and policy change will overcome those barriers. Obviously, the availability of computers also varies from country to country. However, governments can make their computers available to their workforce during non-working hours for educational purposes and this might greatly help public employees to get an MPA education in many places in the world.

Another implication of web-based education is the possibility of sharing top talent in teaching public administration. For example, a well recognized expert can prepare a given course and students in all parts of the state or world can take that course. One of the realities of web-based instruction using the asynchronous discussion board is that it takes time to monitor correctly. Thus, an ideal class or section size is about 24 students. Nevertheless, classes can be huge if universities use well developed course materials and course "tutors" to monitor the discussion boards and grade the essay material. Class preparation is much more difficult but a teacher on video can teach to thousands if his or her school or university uses course tutors for daily and weekly communication with the students under the direction of a senior teacher.

The use of the term online tutor or e-tutor is becoming more common place, especially in Great Britain. These online course tutors rarely have face to face contact with students but are still responsible for providing academic support to groups of students while they are studying a particular course. Philip Barker and Shirley Bennett and Debra Marsh explain the development of this new role in higher education and some of the challenges associated with this new position. The productivity implications in higher education are remarkable because course tutors would not be paid at the same pay rates as tenured or senior professors. This would require a whole new approach to teaching especially in universities but the result would be lower costs for higher education while improving the teaching quality. Not only would labor costs be lower but building costs for classrooms would also be lower. At a time when higher education has become a major cost to government, web-based education spells cost relief.

However, the real advantage comes from team teaching across universities and schools. In many countries, the needed talented professors are not hired because of cost or insufficient labor pool. The web-based approach means that one or more professors can build and even tailor a course for several sets of students in various countries. Peers can evaluate the online course, including the lectures, and can suggest improvements that better fit the targeted students. The teaching product would improve as the feedback for improvements is more easily accomplished. This approach permits cross national talent teams to create courses for students at a much lower per student cost. Thus, the talent of the world can be brought to each place in the world at an affordable cost for the students and governments that help fund the education programs.

Constructivist Use of Web

The arrival of the World Wide Web signals the beginning of some fundamental changes in how teaching, training, and self-directed learning will occur at all ages and stages of life. The World Wide Web as a vehicle for disseminating course materials and for creating active learning experiences within a classroom-based course. Educators at all levels, from Kindergarten to adult training, are drawing a distinction between two fundamentally different approaches to teaching. In one, the goal is to transfer, as effectively and efficiently as possible, a concise and coherent block of information from the teacher or computer into the minds of the learners. Most existing computer-based training for adults has been designed with knowledge transfer in mind. Extraneous information is left out. The emphasis is on individual learning and learners have a limited number of paths through the lesson. This approach works well for the training of basic skills in areas of knowledge that are well defined and stable. For most of us, though, the world just isn't that way. As adults we face one ill-defined problem after another. The specific facts that we have to know change so quickly that some knowledge becomes obsolete almost as soon as we master it. The knowledge-transfer approach doesn't prepare us well for a messy world in constant motion.

An alternative way to think about teaching and learning is called constructivism. A constructivist trainer doesn't strip away the natural complexity of a subject. Instead, multiple perspectives are brought to bear. The goal of a constructivist learning environment is not the accurate transfer of content from the instructor to the learner. Instead, the learner is given tasks and opportunities, information resources and support, and is encouraged to construct their own version of the content, subject to revision through feedback. Many paths through the lesson are allowed and collaboration with other learners is stressed over lonely individual learning. A constructivist use of technology presents information to the learner in multiple forms from multiple sources and invites the learner to make sense of it. The learner can acquire the information needed from several sources via the computer, and from off-line sources including his or her own prior experience, from information gathered while collaborating with other learners, and from references and other sources of expertise found somewhere far away from the computer screen.

A constructivist approach is more learner-focused, and less teacher-focused. The emphasis is on making a set of tasks and resources available to learners, and creating an environment in which the learners can actively create their own meaning in that context, rather than to passively absorb knowledge structures created by the instructor. In this approach, the instructor's role moves toward being a coach and orchestrator of resources, and moves away from being the sole source of information. The emphasis is on cases studies, problem solving, and the creation of meaning.

In the last two years, a new technology has grown enormously in importance and accessibility. This technology, the World Wide Web, lends itself beautifully to constructivist, active learning. The World Wide Web is a part - the fastest growing part - of the internet. In 1989, a group of scientists at the European Laboratory for Particle Physics (CERN) in Geneva, Switzerland began developing an Internet tool that would link information produced by all of the CERN researchers. The tool provided a way to link textual information on different computers and created by different scientists. The object was to overcome issues of incompatibility and utilize a new way of linking made possible by computers, called "hypertext". Rather than presenting information in a linear or hierarchical fashion, hypertext permits information to be linked in a web-like structure.

Nodes of information can be linked to other nodes of information in multiple ways. As a result, users can dynamically criss-cross the information web using pieces in the order most convenient to them. The CERN project resulted in an innovative front-end to the Internet, now referred to as the World-Wide Web (WWW). The WWW provides users with a uniform and convenient means of accessing the vast resources of the Internet. In 1993, the National Center for Supercomputing Applications (NCSA) at the University of Illinois pushed the CERN scientists' idea further by creating a software tool called Mosaic. Mosaic is an easy to use graphical user interface that permits text, graphics, sound and video to be hyperlinked. Mosaic was the first of the Internet tools that are now referred to as " Web browsers". Other well-known browsers include Netscape (the first commercial browser developed by some of the programmers involved with the Mosaic project) and Microsoft's Internet Explorer.

Web browsers permit users to connect to the Internet and facilitate accessing information located on another remote computer. The Web browser links to the remote computer just long enough so that the information you need can be sent to your computer for you to view. Documents created to be viewed by a browser are formatted using Hypertext Markup Language (HTML). HTML solves incompatibility problems by using standardized tags which indicate such things as whether a piece of text should be plain, bold, italic, or linked to another piece of text. Pages of information on a computer formatted with HTML and accessible to someone with a Web browser, are referred to as "home pages" or "Web pages".

The WWW and Web browsers have made the Internet a more user-friendly environment. The ability to integrate graphics, text, and sound into a single tool means that novice users do not have to struggle with such a steep learning curve. In addition, organizations and individuals can create home pages independently and link to other home pages on their own computers or to pages created by others on different computer systems. For educators, the WWW provides an exciting new opportunity for distance teaching and learning. The WWW can be used by the distance educator to build a classroom home page. The home page can cover information about the class including the syllabus, exercises, literature references, and instructor's biography. The instructor can also provide links to information on the WWW that would be useful to students in the class. Other links can access library catalogs or each student's individual home page. In addition, the home page can link students to a discussion list or listserv that set up for student communication. It is also a relatively simple matter to use the homepage to create forms that students can fill out and that will end up being sent to you as an e-mail message.

A web server can be run on a personal computer or a UNIX workstation. The server need not be a fast, expensive machine. In fact, I set up my first server on a six year old Macintosh SE/30. When the traffic grew to the point of justifying the investment, we upgraded to a faster machine. Setting up a server is a fairly simple task, and corporations, university departments, and even elementary schools are doing it every day. What makes the World Wide Web especially exciting is that it also allows you to create anchors that download files for you or allow you to send e-mail to an individual. The web thus makes it easy to gain access to data, software and people. It's a user-friendly front end to almost everything on the internet. Within a year or so, the mechanics of creating documents on the web will become transparent.

Most publishers of word processing software are adding the capability of saving documents in web format to their ever-growing list of features. So far, however, the end result of using a word processor to create web pages directly may not be exactly what you had in mind. An active webwriter will want to know how to tweak the appearance of the documents and, for the moment, that requires some familiarity with HTML. HTML, or HyperText Markup Language, is easy to learn. To prepare a page for the web, you just embed special characters or tags in your document to tell your browser how to display a given word. For a computer trainer, learning the basics of HTML should take no longer than a weekend. Excellent resources for learning HTML can be found on the web, and are indexed in A Primer for Creating Web Resources. The Web 66 Internet Server Cookbook contains recipes for putting pictures and sounds in your pages, serving downloadable files, and maintaining a server from a distance.

An alternative method for displaying content on the web is the Adobe Acrobat format. This allows complex page layouts to be used, but users of your materials must all have the proper helper application installed on their machines. In a corporate environment with software standards in place, this shouldn't be a problem. Once you have created your pages, you simply upload them to the server you'll be using. Most medium to large-sized corporations have already established a web presence, and many smaller companies have as well. Whether you purchase space on the machines of an internet provider or set up your own webserver, you need not be physically near the server itself. Most maintenance can be done from a distance. Once the use of the web as a way to distribute course materials is second nature to you, the next phase is to take advantage of all the material that's out there beyond the walls of your institution.

The more you incorporate such activities into your course, the more it will become transformed into an learner-centered environment and the less often you'll find yourself holding forth on center stage. If you can get friends and colleagues, both in and outside of your enterprise, to volunteer to answer questions, you've broadened the pool of experience available to your students. Newsgroups provide an invisible college of people helping people. They are a great source of up to the minute news about software releases, bugs, and workarounds. If you have your own newsserver, you can also set up internal newsgroups specific to your course to provide a space for students to exchange information on an ongoing basis. Most newsgroups maintain a list of frequently asked questions that have come up within that group. These can be a rich source of materials and pointers to other resources on the web. Most major software publishers (e.g., Microsoft, Novell, Claris, Adobe) have placed their technical notes on the web.

Patches, applications, utilities, documentation... there are many sources of useful wares ready to be downloaded. FTPing (i.e., grabbing) and decompressing this software is handled transparently by your web browser. You can place an anchor on a page that refers to a file and all your users have to do is click on it to have it delivered to their desktop. Suppose you're teaching a course on desktop publishing and you want your students to have the experience of dealing with a difficult client. One way to bring that kind of encounter into the classroom is to set up an e-mail address with a fabricated name. Periodically, you answer the mail at that account while acting like someone else.

Utilize information that already has been developed for your course. If you already have your notes and syllabi in word processed form, make use of tools such as HotDog to format them for distribution on the WWW. Hundreds of home pages have already been developed for courses. Some of these home pages allow students to complete an entire course from the WWW and others are developed in conjunction with lectures delivered on-campus or by video or audio. Utilizing a consistent format for each of your pages. Based on suggestions made by the above mentioned style manuals, develop a consistent format for each web page. While colored or patterned backgrounds can be used on homepages, plain grey or white backgrounds make text easier to read. Keeping page lengths short. Your main index should jump to a lot of shorter pages. In cases where page information is long, index internally so that the student can jump to specific information as needed. Maximizing links to internal information and minimizing links to external information. The purpose of your home page is to provide information on a specific subject area. Only provide external links to home pages that provide useful related information for your students.

The home page should help your students to find necessary course information, learn the material, and get involved in thinking about the course material. Properly designed home pages will encourage thought, discussion and active participation by your distant students. The following elements can be included in your class home page:

— *Course & Instructor Information* — Include such items as course topics to be covered, your office hours, textbook information, course objectives, and grading policies.

— *Class Communication* — Provide access to your e-mail, link to discussion groups that you have set up for student-to-student communication, and create forms that your students can use to report problems or provide biographical information about themselves.

— *Assignments and Tests* — Distribute assignments and tests, provide for online completion or submission, and give solutions, hints, or samples of what you expect.

— *Material covered in the classroom* — Make lecture notes and handouts available either as web pages or as downloadable files.

— *Demonstrations, Animation, Video, Audio* — This is more complex than other suggestions and will require that your students have access to computers with sound and video cards.

— *Reference Material* — List materials in print and electronic form that supplement the textbook. To avoid copyright problems, electronic articles should either be written by you or in the public domain. In addition, provide links to other pages which cover information on the topic, similar courses that may also be available on WWW, your university library, and other on-campus resources that may help your student complete the course.

For many people who are new to the web, the temptation to browse and pursue one link after another is so strong that they spend countless hours glued to the screen. In an educational or training situation, however, we don't have the luxury of spending all of our time that way. As much as we value curiosity and exploration, it's necessary for us to find ways to get the greatest learning benefit from the web in the shortest possible time. At San Diego State University we've been thinking about how to do that, and one lesson format that we've developed toward that goal is called a WebQuest. A WebQuest is an activity of guided inquiry in which learners are given a task which requires internet access to complete.

WebQuests can be designed as short- or long-term activities. At the end of a short term WebQuest, a learner will have grappled with a significant amount of new information and made sense of it. A short-term WebQuest is designed to be completed in one to three class periods. WebQuests are deliberately designed to make the best use of a learner's time. There is questionable educational benefit in having learners surf the net without a clear task in mind, and most educational and training institutions must ration student connect time severely.

Web-Technology and Educational Networks

New technologies with new applications can significantly reduce the costs of school networking and significantly improve the networking capabilities available to students, teachers, and the general public. These economies will make it possible to provide universal access to educational networks, thereby advancing the causes of educational equity and school reform and ending the isolation of the traditional classroom. During the last few years, thousands of schools and hundreds of thousands of students and teachers have begun to develop the Internet into a major educational resource. Within the community of educational researchers, the Internet is now an accepted standard. Network use is also growing rapidly throughout the larger educational community, but several factors have placed practical limits on this growth. Consider first some of the reasons that propel educational use of the Internet. These include the following:

— *Isolation*: Wide-area computer networks can help end the isolation of students and teachers in the traditional classroom. Of course, networks will accomplish this end only if they are inexpensive enough to be made available to all students and teachers.

— *Equity*: Connecting all schools to the Internet will provide equity of access to online information and create opportunities for all schools to publish online. This requires a reasonably priced infrastructure that all schools can afford to purchase, install, and maintain.

— *Reform:* Networks can be a powerful tool in support of educational reform. A widespread network infrastructure with easy access to information servers and tools for placing resources on servers will allow students, classes, and teachers to produce online materials, do extensive collaborative work, and broadly share instructional resources.

Schools face possible obstacles in each of these areas. If a school cannot obtain adequate connectivity, its ability to overcome isolation will be limited. If it has no access to a server, its ability to publish materials online will be limited. If it has too few user devices for all students to participate in networking activities, the promise of equity will not be achieved. And if tools do not exist that enable students and teachers to use networks imaginatively and effectively to support their broader educational goals, the promise of educational reform will not be met. Overcoming each of these obstacles entails a technological challenge.

Networking is a means of building community, and a strong sense of community is often the key to building viable network-linked educational programs and resources and sustaining them over the long term. The types of educational and community networks that we advocate differ in some essential ways from those developed for many commercial applications. Commercial networks emphasize privacy and security issues over cost and access considerations. For educational and community networks, cost and access are the primary concerns, and network architectures that neglect these factors are unlikely to be sustainable for very long. Shared infrastructure and broad applicability bring other educational benefits. They create network environments that are conducive to interdisciplinary and collaborative activities and to research projects that explore an ever-expanding scope of resources. We believe that these sorts of activities and projects can contribute effectively to educational reform. We find that the portions of networks with the highest development costs and the greatest need for cost reduction are precisely those with the fewest possibilities for shared infrastructure. To put the issue in colloquial terms, we must deal not so much with the problem of building the information superhighway as with building the information driveway that leads into the home or classroom. Once this part of network connectivity is established, there remains the task of using it effectively to access online material and produce materials for others to use.

Two factors dramatically affect the performance and affordability of internetworking: the cost and bandwidth of the 'local loop' from the user's site to the nearest network point of presence, and the existence of a complementary wide-area infrastructure to tie the various local loops together. These two factors are critical regardless of the specific details of the chosen technology or the market position of the service provider. Schools and communities should choose their network technologies and services strategically, with an eye toward how their choices will support and leverage the overall networking infrastructure. Broad infrastructure needs are a much more important consideration in developing educational and community networks than in planning private networks or networks that serve a limited number of public or nonprofit organisations. Even though educational programs have a specific focus, they inspire other activities, and they rely on other organisations for many kinds of resources. Hence, it is important to consider the entire community as a unit when assessing alternatives for providing an economical infrastructure for school or community networking.

Several factors make it likely that the costs of providing connectivity will drop, perhaps dramatically, in the next few years. One strong influence is market competition to supply the local loop. Where there are multiple suppliers of connectivity to schools, homes, or offices, competitive forces will help reduce the cost of network services to these sites. Many communities are experiencing active competition in this area, although recent federal telecommunications legislation may allow the reestablishment of monopolies of local connectivity, with a corresponding decrease in options and likely increase in price. One must also take care to distinguish competition in the local loop from competition in limited market segments, such as voice or video services. While this latter form of competition could decrease the price of specific services, it may have no relevance to data services and internetworking. More typically, some service providers may engage in 'cream-skimming'—seeking to exploit market segments with the highest profit margins, a practice which public utility commissions and local regulatory authorities should probably discourage. Tariff policies also affect the viability of various options for Internet access. For example, the commonly available digital telephone service known as ISDN can provide economical connectivity at moderate bandwidths, as long as its tariffs are set at an affordable flat rate (with no time charges). When time charges are applied, this service becomes uneconomical for typical network interconnects, since it is desirable to keep the connection in place throughout the day.

Competition to provide local loops is likely to involve a number of new technologies. Telephone subscribers can employ new electronics—most notably, a technology known in telephonic circles as High-bit-rate Digital Subscriber Loop (HDSL)—to wring vastly higher data rates out of older copper infrastructure. HDSL can provide data services at speeds in excess of one megabit per second and costs as low as one-tenth those of traditional connections. Public utility commissions will ultimately determine whether these economies result in savings for home, school, and office subscribers or in larger profits for telephone companies. This is a complex issue, since rates are determined not only by the intrinsic cost of any single service to the telephone company, but also by the fraction of equipment and maintenance left in the hands of the customer, the need to subsidize certain lifeline services, and the need to average rates across the many different technologies used to supply local loops for a given region. In addition to HDSL, which provides a symmetrical service, there are also asymmetrical services, such as Asymmetric Digital Subscriber Loop (ADSL).

Symmetrical services provide the same data rate into and out of a given site.

Asymmetrical services typically provide higher data rates into a given site than out of it. While asymmetrical services may be acceptable for a residence, where the users are mostly consumers of information, they would not be appropriate for connections to local area networks at schools and libraries because they would limit the ability to publish information at these sites. And although some ADSL technologies have much higher bandwidths than HDSL, they provide significantly higher speeds only in the forward (outward) direction, and they cannot drive data for the distances that HDSL can. A new service known as SDSL promises to offer the bandwidth advantages of ADSL in a symmetrical mode. Another promising development in the field of telephony is the deployment of fiber optics, either to drop points in the neighborhood or to the curbside of subscriber homes or offices. Fiber brings vastly higher bandwidth than copper and promises higher reliability over time.

Once the capital costs of laying this new infrastructure are depreciated, suppliers can anticipate significant reductions in the costs of providing high bandwidth data services, namely those with speeds in excess of one million bits per second. Such services would exhaust only a tiny fraction of the bandwidth available through a fiber infrastructure, which can also provide video services requiring the equivalent of tens of millions of bits per second. Some telephone companies are contemplating a fiber optic/coaxial cable hybrid system, an architecture commonly used by newer cable television installations. These systems provide a particularly attractive architecture for data services and internetworking: they can offer services with peak bandwidths of 10 to 40 million bits per second or higher, at prices potentially competitive with those of present-day analog telephone service. Widespread deployment of such systems will help redefine the pricing structure for high-bandwidth data services, as prices drop as low as a few percent of current service offerings.

With extensive deployment, the cable modems needed to deliver this service can be marketed at prices comparable to those of conventional modems, and the service itself can be sold for prices comparable to those of premium cable channels. Where internal wiring is costly to install and where external connectivity is difficult to achieve through fixed links, wireless technologies offer an attractive option. With its ease of setup, wireless is particularly appealing in situations where costly and time-consuming building modifications are necessary to install internal wiring. Wireless links can also be used to provide pieces of a metropolitan area network infrastructure. But one must bear in mind that maintenance costs for wireless links are likely to be higher than those for fixed wiring and that the bandwidth available for wireless communications is extremely limited compared to the bandwidth of fixed copper or fiber infrastructure. This important point has been largely overlooked by groups advocating wireless technologies as a panacea for public network access. These technologies offer an excellent starting point for such access, but as usage grows, the bandwidth available through this medium will inevitably become saturated, and the majority of public Internet traffic will have to be transferred to traditional fixed communications links. Thus, there will have to be truly compelling reasons to deploy wireless communications between fixed points in a metropolitan area.

Wireless technologies can be used effectively, however, as a rapid enabler, a temporary connection that can serve a networking purpose while fixed wiring is being planned and installed. Upon completion of wiring, the wireless apparatus might be reused to help leverage another start-up site. New technologies are also generating new means of tying together local loops to form a wide-area networking infrastructure. New telephone architectures offer the possibility of significantly reduced costs for data services and internetworking. The traditional telephone infrastructure connects lines from homes and offices to switches at the telephone company's central offices, forming circuits through which telephone calls are routed. This circuit-switched infrastructure is oriented toward point-to-point connections, with endpoints that may be very widely separated. Each connection ties up switch and transmission resources for the duration of the connection, regardless of how much information is being passed through the circuit. Internet services are based upon a quite different architecture, one that involves a common 'cloud' of connectivity through which individual data packets are routed to their final destinations. This packet-switched infrastructure offers a number of significant advantages for data transmission.

Individual circuits need not be maintained, so there are lower costs in terms of switches and infrastructure relating to the transmission plant. Demands are made upon this infrastructure only during the actual transmission of data packets. Furthermore, thanks to the manner in which Internet protocols behave in the presence of traffic congestion, the system can be overloaded briefly with only a slowdown in the rate of data transmission as opposed to a failure to establish a desired connection. This type of packet-switched infrastructure can be provided through a number of technologies commonly offered by the telephone industry and referred to collectively as 'fast packet services.' The optimal mix of technologies will depend upon local pricing and needs. More important than specific programmatic needs may be the overall strategies employed to provide connectivity to schools and community centers in a given area.

Connectivity alone does not create a networked environment of value to schools and communities. More important is the quality of information available over the network and the ability of schools and communities to use the network as their own publishing venue. Determining the costs of such services requires an analysis of the costs of the client and server machines and the availability of software suitable to provide these services. We consider first the question of client machines or access devices. Computers can be bought now for $1,000 to $2,000. This has been true for the last half-dozen years, and it is likely to remain true as long as the only forces governing these prices are traditional computer marketplace forces. It is not the price of the raw materials or the manufacturing cost that determines the retail price of personal computers. Rather, marketing strategies and advertising decisions set these prices. Producing a $200 user device capable of running a World Wide Web browser over standard telephone links is within the realm of possibility, provided that a large enough market exists for such a device.

Many forces are converging to make it likely that such devices will be produced. These include the progress of game machines, which now typically contain powerful graphics computers as a standard component, the development of set-top boxes for cable television systems, and the need of schools for large numbers of cheap, networked computers. With the rapid evolution of computer hardware, operating systems, and software, it is possible to pass still-serviceable hardware from business and government offices into the hands of schools and community groups, who could use it to gain basic Internet access at extremely low cost. The advent of Windows 95, with its significant new hardware demands, is beginning to drive many commercial users to invest in new hardware. But much of the remaindered hardware is still capable of running the older Windows operating system and supporting graphical interfaces to Internet resources. If commercial users donated remaindered hardware to schools and community centers, and if mechanisms to support this hardware were put in place, it might be possible to rapidly provide network access to all of the nation's classrooms.

There are many uncertainties associated with such a scheme. It assumes that the evolution of software for classroom application will be much slower than the evolution of commercial software, so that the Windows machines will be adequate for most educational applications for a number of years. And it assumes that new features in commercial software will not make the training that students receive with older machines and software irrelevant to the commercial workplace.

Finally, it assumes that older machines can be supplied in quantities sufficient to provide school districts with a uniform and supportable computing environment. If these conditions can be met, the donation of older equipment could provide a significant boost to school and community networking efforts. This is only an interim approach and a partial solution for school and community networking, but it should allow communities to stretch significantly the dollars available for networking projects. Whether the client machines are standard office computers or low-cost school and home computers, they will require affordable client software in order to access common information services. Under one widely used marketing model that works to the advantage of educational users, software vendors charge a fee for their server software but give away client software free of charge to all users or, more commonly, to educational users.

The rationale for this pricing model is that it encourages access to online information, for which there may be an access fee. Vendors may also charge a fee for the construction of servers to groups that place information online for commercial access. Under this type of pricing arrangement, it is possible for educational users to obtain high quality World Wide Web and Geographical Information System browsers, among others. The practical consequence is that the client code is free to educational users but is well-maintained to insure the availability of solid code for all commercial clients. Whether the market will continue to support this type of pricing structure depends largely on whether the majority of vendors adhere to standards for transporting information over the network. If large volumes of material are available through a small set of common standard protocols, there are likely to be low-cost or free products available to implement these standards. If one vendor obtains a near monopoly on the market, there is a danger of that vendor introducing proprietary protocols in its products and forcing educational users to purchase them at arbitrarily high prices. We would regard this as a classic monopoly situation that could be addressed under existing antitrust laws.

On the server side, there is a relatively broad range of options, consistent with the idea that one need support only a small set of network protocols to supply a very wide range of information services. With an increasing number of vendors supplying Internet servers for school use, we are fast approaching the possibility of a generic Internet server. Generic servers can be built on the most common hardware platforms with public domain operating systems at a fraction of the cost of servers commonly available just a year or two ago. Current networking projects and forthcoming network products are likely to produce enough examples of server setup and maintenance to make their operation practical in any school or school district. Further simplification of this task will occur as new software is developed to facilitate the management of these machines, both locally at the school site and remotely from a district office or contracted system management provider. Some vendors provide free client software but extract a fee, sometimes a very large one, for the server software. Fortunately, many vendors are adjusting server charges based on the features offered and the audience likely to use them. For example, systems that include advanced security features for financial transactions are likely to be sold at higher prices than systems meant for simpler information delivery systems. Here, too, adherence to a small set of network protocols makes it likely that low-cost or free implementation of information services will be available to educational and community networks. It is important to realise that services like the World Wide Web have their limitations, too, and to consider mechanisms that will help overcome these limitations for educational and community users. Advances are also being made in the area of Web editors, which simplify the task of creating resources to be placed online via the World Wide Web. These advances are reducing the costs of training students and teachers to create multimedia presentations for online distribution and increasing their ability to develop these resources as part of their standard classroom activities. A number of vendors have announced products in this area.

Two important tasks must be accomplished in order to extend internet access to all students and teachers and enable them to incorporate internet resources and techniques into their everyday educational activities. Schools and homes must be provided with connectivity, and second, facilities must be developed that make it easy and inexpensive to create and access online resources. We believe that technologies exist to meet these goals—indeed, we believe that the ideals of universal connectivity for all the nation's classrooms and commonplace classroom use of the Internet can be realized by the end of the decade.

Multiculturality of World Wide Web

The World Wide Web has introduced a new collection of educational opportunities for educators and students. But where there are new opportunities, they are usually accompanied by a series of new challenges. While training programs and instructional materials have made it easier for teachers to use the Internet more effectively in the classroom, recent research has shown that teachers still identify a lack of knowledge about the Internet as the primary reason they have not used it more often as a teaching tool. More challenges arise when teachers do become cyber-savvy. For example, information on the Web is not static. People who run Web servers usually do not screen Web site creators' credibility or qualifications on their site's content. This calls into question the accuracy and credibility of many Web sites. When explored with a set of strategies that address these challenges, the World Wide Web has the potential to transcend the capabilities of many other multicultural media in its supplemental value to multicultural teaching practices.

The key for unlocking this potential lies in understanding and using the Web not merely as an enormous compendium of informational resources, but more importantly as an interactive medium that can connect people across borders and boundaries. With this in mind, there are clear intersections between some of the important ideals in multicultural curriculum transformation and the educational opportunities presented by the Web. A vast network of teachers and students around the world and across myriad cultures who have read a particular textbook, gathering somewhere to share questions and exchange resources on a given topic. The interactive opportunities can transcend the potential of most other educational media as a means to connect students with first person sources beyond classroom walls and national borders and across cultures. Most Web site creators provide an email address and/or other contact information so that teachers, students, and others can, in fact, contact them with questions, challenges, critiques, or comments.

Many educators understand Inclusive teaching as incorporating diverse voices and perspectives in the classroom. To them, inclusion is about finding materials and tools that are representative of the students in the classroom. Multicultural education takes this concept a step further. If education is truly to be student-centered, then the experiences, perspectives, and ideas of the students themselves must be brought to the fore in the educational experience. To be "included" in the educational process, students, as well as teachers, must be given opportunities to have their voices heard and to hear each others' voices.

The Web is helping to facilitate this kind of inclusivity through countless sites that encourage teachers and students to participate in virtual global communities with other teachers and students who may be either very culturally similar or different. Collaborative and interdisciplinary teaching and learning are concepts that have been introduced, attempted, and reintroduced for decades. It is not uncommon for a group of teachers from a particular school to combine efforts in an attempt to connect lessons from subject to subject. In fact, for many teachers who struggle with time constraints and burn-out, sharing resources and collaborative planning become vital aspects of day-to-day classroom operations. For others, it is an avenue for modeling constructive and cooperative bridge-building across groups. As with Interactive and Inclusive teaching and learning, the Web has the potential to greatly expand the breadth and depth of collaborative possibilities of educators.

Despite the wonderful multicultural and educational potential the Internet holds, the very feature of the Internet that can facilitate Interactive, Collaborative, and Inclusive teaching and learning - interactivity - remains sadly untapped by educators. Like no previous medium, the Internet can facilitate cross-cultural communication, interpersonal bridge-building, and intercultural networking. It can expand your resource base virtually infinitely and diversify it to a previously unthinkable extent. Below are some strategies for using the Internet to do just that - expand your resource base by networking across cultures, national boundaries, and even comfort zones. Several email discussion forums exist that deal specifically with multicultural education and related issues. Participants can post messages to a list address, and those messages are then circulated to the rest of the forum's subscribers via email. Like discussion boards, email forums provide participants with the opportunity to network with other people interested in a particular topic and to engage in challenging and thought-provoking dialogue on a variety of issues.

Email forums tend to be more intimate and personal than discussion boards. Because people generally participate in email forums over a considerable length of time, the names and email addresses flashing into everyone's mailbox can become familiar. This can provide an opportunity to make more personal connections with other educators or activists from around the world. Several recent studies indicate that the primary reason teachers give for not incorporating computer technology into classroom practice is a lack of training or knowledge about how to use products such as CD-ROMs and Web sites. Educators, already pressured by time constraints, are often intimidated by a perceived learning curve when it comes to developing better computer skills. For many, this feeling is exacerbated when they finally learn enough about the Web to navigate around cyberspace and do simple searches, and suddenly find themselves lost in a maze of broken links, pornographic sites, and educational sites that have little or no original content or that have not been updated since 1996.

Several media and educational organizations are familiar for producing TV shows, films, CD-ROMs, books, and other teaching and learning materials that support multicultural ideals and curriculum development. The National Geographic Society, the Discovery Channel, the Public Broadcasting Company (PBS) and others have been part of many of our classrooms for years. Like other educational organizations and companies, National Geographic, PBS, and others recognize that in order to remain competitive in today's market, they need to include a strong and visible Web presence among their multiple projects. As a result, they have developed a series of techniques and strategies for attracting Web users to their sites. One strategy many organizations employ to bring users to their sites is to provide free educational materials and resources. In fact, there seems to be a competition brewing among those companies known for producing educational media to offer more, and better, resources than their competitors. Teachers and students are among the winners of this competition, reaping the benefits of several sites scrambling to outdo their competitors.

Companies that are already known for producing quality educational materials have a vested interest in offering only well-researched and well-evaluated resources. So one simple strategy for digging through the dirt to find quality classroom resources on the Web quickly is to turn directly to the Web sites of National Geographic Society, the Discovery Channel, and others who have a reputation for producing effective educational media and whose products have been proven effective in your classroom.

In many cases, these sites offer entire sections such as "Teaching Tools" or "Lesson Plans" or "Student Resources." Many actually host online learning activities for students and discussion forums for educators. Some allow you to download a variety of educational materials including maps, audio and video clips, worksheets, and historical documents. And again, companies who have built reputations by producing and supporting quality educational projects and resources know that it is in their best interest to provide only high quality resources through the Web. There seem to be hundreds of "Multicultural Education Links" pages or general multicultural education pages that are comprised entirely of links to other sites. What makes these sites confusing and frustrating is that they are often linked to each other. A user can spend hours linking from one list of links to another, and so on, without ever finding original resources, teaching tools, or interactive opportunities. Most of the criteria used to assess and evaluate traditional educational media such as textbooks and films can be directly applied to Web sites as well. These include: accuracy of the information, critical analysis of possible bias, credibility of the author and/or publishing source, appropriateness and accessibility to the specified audience, timeliness, relevance to a particular subject area, validity of content, and effectiveness of aesthetic aspects. Still, for a variety reasons, even deeper considerations for some of the more traditional educational evaluation criteria and several new criteria must be added to old models to holistically evaluate products of this fairly new cyber-medium.

For instance, unlike traditional educational media such as films, textbooks, and journals that usually go through a rigorous review process before being made widely available to teachers and students, virtually anybody with access to a Web server can create an educational Web site. In most cases, there is no entity comparable to a publishing company to help ensure the credibility or expertise of educational Web designers. Likewise, as is the case with many journals, there is no formal review board to examine the validity of the information on most educational Web sites. For the most part, the responsibility is left with the user to assess these issues.

Other complications to the assessment of Web sites exist within the structure of the medium itself. In no other medium is the line between commercial and informational distinctions quite so blurry. Sometimes it is difficult to ascertain whether a particular site is a purely commercial venture or a purely educational venture. In fact, it might well be the case that no site fits the latter extreme. Again, since many Web sites are produced by unfamiliar sources, we, the users, must look deeper to uncover the bias of an educational Web site. In addition, unlike in books or films, the information on Web sites is not static. This can be a strength, allowing site maintainers and authors to continually update material. Literally hundreds of models for evaluating Web sites have been created by university librarians, educational and instructional technologists, and Web developers. Some of these focus on content credibility and validity while others focus on design and navigability. There is sometimes a tendency in education to use new technology for the sake of using new technology and without a particular need or sense for how it will improve curricula or pedagogy. As somewhat of a cautionary measure, this category may appear to be an obvious first step in assessing a Web site or any educational product. It explores the extent to which the content and target audience of a site match with your needs and target audience.

Criticisms of Web-based Education

Some of the more common criticisms of web-based education are listed below.

1. The academy has not conducted a thorough research on the efficacy of learning online. With this argument, we would not implement any innovation. This argument tells us not to implement this innovation until the academy and policy makers are confident that this new innovation will live up to its promises. This is a cry normally heard when a major innovation starts to happen. The answer is also normal. Certainly, due caution is necessary but this should not be a reason for stopping innovation. Try it and see what happens on a more limited basis. If it works, expand its use. If it does not work, then stop the implementation.

2. The academy has not prepared professors to teach online classes. In any innovation, the first stage sees innovators that are willing to experiment without proper assistance or guidance. Ideally, professors

should be compensated for their time and effort the first time they prepare such classes. Ideally, a full technical support staff should exist to assist the professors and even teach the professors what to do. Hopefully, such support will occur at the better universities but many will just do the best that they can. As more and more professors have experience with web-based education, they can share their knowledge and provide then needed teaching expertise in seminars and training sessions.

3. With web-based education, the academy has adopted an entrepreneurial desire for economic gain rather than the desire to support through acquisition of knowledge thorough rigorous education. Clearly, many institutions of higher learning will see web-based education as a means to increase revenue and that will motivate their decision rather than providing rigorous education. However, this does mean that web-based education is not a means to provide quality rigorous education. Although different, web-based education can be as rigorous as traditional teaching. For many public universities suffering from budget constraints or a mandate to teach a wide geographic area, web-based education may be the only viable alternative that provides a quality professional education.

The cure for abuse (accreditation and the market place) is the same cure that exists in traditional education. For example in the United States, the National Association of Schools of Public Administration and Affairs can and should establish accreditation guidelines for online courses and web-based MPA programs. The other classic cure is the market place where students and employers seek out places that offer quality education regardless if is traditional or web-based. Those universities that do not offer a good product will not attract students and employers will not wish to employ students from those programs.

4. Web-based education is biased against liberal learning that requires a give and take communication between and among students and the teacher. Those who argue for liberal learning say it is "one of the primary means through which individuals develop their own personhood, and such development has as its foundational value and goal the freedom whereby students make choices that contribute to their personal well-being". Is web-based education impossible for the teacher who wishes to pursue liberal learning? The answer is a simple NO. This approach to education is just as possible with webbased education as it is in traditional education. Certainly, the means for teaching liberal learning vary from traditional education, but they exist. Several large research consortia exist that are developing the programs and algorithms that will improve the technology to perform all the interactive activies to support a liberal education.

5. The online approach eliminates the value of personal relationships in the name of efficiency and students can no longer question the authority of the teacher because they cannot argue a position until its weaknesses are exposed in classroom dialogue. The web-based education discussion board, chat room, and email list serve provide the means for a teacher to develop these characteristics in students. Certainly, the teacher can choose not to use these tools but the traditional classroom teacher can also halt any classroom discussion. Again, the accomplishment of this teaching objective is purely a function of the teacher and not the vehicle used by the teacher.

Socialization of students into a professional culture has always been and must remain a great concern of a quality MPA programs. Technology can help to accomplish that socialization by using a combination of personnel web pages, email, posted student photographs, and posted videos.

However, an online MPA program can also require students to visit the main campus two or three times during the 18 to 24 month program. For example, upon entry into the program, the MPA program can require students to take a computer lab on how to use the computer but also provide socialization activities to make sure that students meet each other and understand the meaning of a professional education. Possibly, in the summers, MPA programs can require students to visit campus to engage in thoughtful retreats, prepare for internships and directed reading assignments, and meet role models of professionalism. Possibly, the programs could require the students to attend a professional conference such as the American Society for Public Administration's national conference as a class and spend time at the conference as a group participating and reflecting on what they were learning from the experience.

6. The online approach merely eliminates a student's literacy because of the over reliance on visual culture (videos, audios, automated quizzes, and so on). This over reliance short circuits the brain development necessary for literacy as well a critical abstract thinking). Web-based education does encourage the teacher to use videos, PowerPoint, and automated quizzes. But the teacher can and should still require the student to read the assignment text material. The teacher can still require critical abstract thinking from

the student in drop box assignments and discussion board forums. Again, the criticism is directed against the teaching of some rather than the medium used for teaching.

7. Sometimes teaching simply requires a face to face discussion between the teacher and the professor in order to make the necessary point with the student. Yes, it does. But again, web-based education really does not prevent this face to face exchange unless it is organized incorrectly. With online and traditional education, a university can (and some universities) do teach classes of over 1,000 students. The occasionally needed face to face interaction just does not exist. However, if the approach to web-based teaching includes dividing a class into small sections of 24 students and using course tutors to manage the sections, then tutors can provide the occasional face to face interactions in person or by using technology such as net meeting. If a rare substantive question occurs beyond the ability of the course tutor, the option always exists to ask the web course preparer.

In summary, teachers can abuse both web-based education and traditional education but both can also provide the necessary quality rigorous education. The reasons for poor teaching remain the same in both approaches: poor instructors and poor educational policies at the university level. Blaming the approach is misdirected.

In any innovation that requires fundamental change, criticisms from those that need to change and do not wish to will be common, as they are searching for reasons not to change. At its logical extreme, web-based education does require radical change and the cries of resistance will be loud. In fact, the very nature of the human condition seems to include resistance to most changes. For example, some still argue against the automobile over driving a horse and carriage. But resistance to innovation does not mean that change should not occur. With resistance to innovation, we need better management, planning, and flexible leadership to not only overcome the resistance but to use the constructive criticism in the resistance to improve the innovation.

Barriers to Web-based Education

In public administration education, the resistance of faculty and the reluctance of higher educational administrators to adapt to this new approach will retard the advancement of web-based education. As noted before, new professors resist this approach because they do not have a secure position. They realize that the full use of this approach to teaching requires them to record their lectures and the development of this type of course requires a great deal more effort and organization on their part.

In traditional courses, non-tenured professors know that tenure committees often make judgments on their teaching performance based almost entirely upon student evaluations. Actual evaluations of their course content teaching materials are rare. Therefore, they focus on preparing entertaining and often relatively less challenging course materials that appeal to students. In web-based courses, non-tenured professors know that tenure committees will make judgments on their teaching performance using the course materials they develop and post online for the world to see. For example, any misstatements and errors are officially "on the record" for the tenure committee to see during the tenure process. Therefore, there is less chance that they will get a positive review under the web-based approach. Being normal intelligent people, they will naturally avoid web-based teaching.

Also, web-based education requires a great deal more effort. Tenure committees judge non-tenured faculty on education, service, and research. The latter normally means publications in peer review journals. If in five or six years, a non-tenured professor does not publish enough, then he or she is out of job. At better universities, the teaching load per semester is lower but the publishing expectation is higher. The reality of web-based teaching is that it requires at least double the amount of time per class if the teacher both prepares and manages the class. The communication (email and discussion board primarily) between the teacher and the professor is much greater in a web-based class than in the traditional class.

In addition, preparation is more complex. In traditional teaching, the professor only needs a syllabus, an extensive set of notes, some tests, and some plan to present the material to the students. In web-based teaching, the professor needs the same as the traditional class; but he or she also needs a complete set of PowerPoint slides that cover the lecture notes, videos of him or her lecturing each PowerPoint presentation, a very large set of objective quizzes with feedback comments on right and wrong answers, and a set of forums for the discussion board. Because the course preparation time is often double that of the traditional class, there is less time available to publish in spite of the fact that publishing expectations are not lowered. Thus, web-based education increases the new professor's risk of perishing in their "publish or perish" world. Tenured professors are also not encouraged to support this method of teaching because of the greater work required, the new required skills and the increased accountability for what is taught. It requires them to learn a whole new set of teaching skills. For example, the professor should learn and use Microsoft Producer. This means the professor needs to master the use of PowerPoint, video presentation, video production, and integration of PowerPoint with the produced videos. Without some form of compensation, either financial or in release time, few tenured faculty are likely to take on the extra work. Once a course is placed on the web, the department chair might wish to see and comment on the professor's work, which before was probably never reviewed unless student complaints warranted it.

Administrators will find web-based education a challenge because the need for technical support and equipment is critical and the whole structure of the academic department will change. In traditional education, the academic department need only ask the library to order books, the facilities people to find classrooms, and secretaries to help faculty type papers and so on. In web-based education, the academic department needs to do all the same things but it must also hire course tutors as adjuncts or instructors to work with senior professors. The senior professors prepare the major online courses and ask the computer support staff to always keep the online course available for students and provide the necessary digital camera equipment and adequate computer capacity. This means that academic department budgets will shift to increasingly pay for less expensive adjuncts and instructors, who will be less qualified and also less committed to the institution and the program than tenure track faculty. This also means department chairs must manage the tension between the more prestigious tenure track faculty and more numerous instructors.

Many new web-based professors may not like that their job now requires administration. In traditional education, the professor might supervise a graduate assistant but essentially the professor did the teaching. In web-based education, the professor must also work with the computer support staff and course tutors. The introduction of new computer technology, the need to keep the course up on the web, and the desire to upgrade the quality of the course materials require the professor to have a strong relationship with the computer support staff. The professor's primary responsibility will shift to preparing and updating the online class materials and the actual daily relationship with the students will fall to the course tutors. The course tutors must also interact with the professor in order to improve the class and clarify any points of confusion over course substance. The relationship with course tutors maybe within the academic department but it can also be a virtual relationship when the course tutor works at other universities that merely contracts with professor to provide the course material.

One simple method to overcome the above barriers is merely to pay the professors extra money to move to online teaching. Given that web-based education actually should increase revenue, the university can use some of the extra money for that purpose. Typically, a university might be willing to pay the professor more money for the extra work of preparation but additional continuing compensation is not likely. However, webbased professors may soon argue that students at other universities and sites take their classes and they should receive higher compensation. Such web-based professors will be in demand and should command larger compensations.

9

Emergence of Web Journalism

Web journalism is defined as the reporting of facts produced and distributed via the World Wide Web. An early leader was The News & Observer in Raleigh, North Carolina. Steve Yelvington wrote on the Poynter Institute website about Nando, owned by The N&O, by saying "Nando evolved into the first serious, professional news site on the World Wide Web — long before CNN, MSNBC, and other followers." It originated in the early 1990s as "NandO Land". Many news organizations based in other media also distribute news online, but the amount they use of the new medium varies. Some news organizations use the Web exclusively or as a secondary outlet for their content. The Online News Association is the premier organization representing online journalists, with more than 800 members.

The Internet challenges traditional news organisations in several ways. Newspapers may lose classified advertising to websites, which are often targeted by interest instead of geography. These organisations are concerned about real and perceived loss of viewers and circulation to the Internet. And the revenue gained with advertising on news websites is sometimes too small to support the site. Even before the Internet, technology and other factors were dividing people's attention, leading to more - but narrower - media outlets.

The Internet has also given rise to more participation by people who aren't normally journalists, such as with Indy Media. Bloggers write on web logs or blogs. Traditional journalists often do not consider bloggers to automatically be journalists. This has more to do with standards and professional practices than the medium. But, as of 2005, blogging has generally gained at least more attention and has led to some effects on mainstream journalism, such as exposing problems related to a television piece about President Bush's National Guard Service. Other significant tools of on-line journalism are Internet forums, discussion boards and chats, especially those representing the Internet version of official media. The widespread use of the Internet all over the world created a unique opportunity to create a meeting place for both sides in many conflicts, such as the Israeli-Palestinian conflict and the Russian-Chechen War. Often this gives a unique chance to find new, alternative solutions to the conflict, but often the Internet is turned into the battlefield by contradicting parties creating endless "online battles."

Most Internet users agree that on-line sources are often less biased and more informative than the official media. This claim is often backed with the belief that on-line journalists are merely volunteers and freelancers who are not paid for their activity, and therefore are free from corporate ethics. But recently many Internet forums began to moderate their boards because of threat of vandalism, which many users see as a form of censorship.

Web journalism provides an abundance of international news. Regardless of where you sit, access to international news has never been better. International news has always been fairly abundant, although frequently dominated by news from the USA. Although this does not completely change in the online environment, the internet brings access to a wide variety of notable international online journalism offerings, or a host of other news sources from all parts of the world.

Although these sources are published in a variety of languages, online resources such as Systran make translation simple and free. Translation is not perfect, but it does competently translate the basic idea. International news is being transformed in the world of the internet and why people around the world, are devouring unprecedented levels of international news, information, and communication about world events and processes. No longer is the audience passive. It has come alive with activity.

People can get their information from literally thousands of news sources around the world. They can get the story from multiple perspectives, placed in rich historical context, and told using a wide variety of communication modalities, not just the one or two available to analog media. For example, audio, video, interactivity, immersive and navigable images, text, hyperlinks, and much more are available online. All of this media richness gives the online audience a more textured and engaging experience and potentially a much fuller understanding of the subtleties and nuances of stories being reported from around the world.

In contrast to the world of analog journalism, the public in the digital age frequently seeks to publish its own views on world events and how media report on them. Internet technology enables audiences anywhere to participate in a global dialogue about world events and issues. Individuals can come into direct contact with one another, though separated by thousands of miles, mountains and oceans, and political and cultural boundaries. The best news providers online are those that, along with their repurposed content, offer original material designed specifically for the web. Many international news sites cover breaking news, and the better sites use their vast reservoirs of space to add depth and texture. The site of *Washington Post* has its own staff of journalists, which gives it the capability to do its own enterprise reporting. *CNN.com*, which is one of the world's busiest websites, with more than 3.5 million page views a day, features extensive original coverage of the environment and ecological issues. It goes into considerable depth on stories that get only a minute or two of treatment in television. *USAToday.com* and *ABCNews.com* are especially effective at supplementing their repurposed content with original graphics, animations, and interactive features.

The *Chicago Tribune* used its website to pay tribute to one of twentieth century journalism's larger figures. The interactive tribute includes 13 news stories about Mike Royko, an electronic message board, and an archive of more than 100 of Royko's best columns. The *Tribune* has also developed an interactive city-based feature called *Digital City*, which it localises at websites of other newspapers in chain. *Digital City* is a direct competitor with Microsoft's *Sidewalk* online city-based service. It offers readers an interactive smattering of news and weather, sports, entertainment, community and marketplace information, and services. The standard for convergence—the coming together of once-separate media in a digital, networked environment—in online journalism was set out by *Boston.com*. The site not only provides an electronic window into Boston's arts, weather, and commerce but offers readers access to the online content of 17 local media. *Wire*, the website introduced in 1996 by the

Associated Press, provides continuously updated breaking news. A number of local, regional, and national websites include direct access to the *Wire*. The pressure to be first, especially in an online arena where real-time news is the standard, can be a threat to accuracy.

According to researches in the field of online journalism, the most popular online journalism is news about information technology, the computer network, which publishes perhaps the premier. A 1997 special report comprehensively reviews CD-ROM drives of every speed and type. The report offers an interactive viewer that enables readers to see how varying speed drives were tested. Readers can customise the report to obtain a graphical display of the drives either alphabetically or from best to worst in terms of a variety of characteristics, including access time, performance, and installation. The site also offers readers customisable downloads of more than one thousand software packages.

Web has produced a set of chic and well-travelled destinations for the digital literati, the best of which not only offer insightful and provocative online discourse but engage readers in interactive discussions and push the storytelling envelope. Some are connected to print publications. One of the most-visited sites is *HotWired,* the electronic version of *Wired* magazine, which features commentary on new media issues as well as new media applications. *Atlantic Unbound,* the online offering of the *Atlantic Monthly,* has offered readers since 1993 an electronic window into politics, society, the arts, and culture, earning a National Magazine Award in new media in 1997. *Salon* not only offers all the traditional intellectual fare of the opinion magazine but features compelling online discussion as well. In *Table Talk,* participants discuss topics ranging from books to digital culture in a tree-and-branch conversation structure based on a model developed at the Well, the first significant online community, born in the spring of 1985. Sports sites on the web may not necessarily raise the journalistic bar, but they are compelling because they so effectively exploit the web's capabilities. *Sports Network* runs a distant second to these premier general-interest sports services and adheres to a more traditional approach to sports reporting with fewer interactive online features. *USAToday* offers good sports coverage as well, but navigation through the site is not as simple as it is in the three premier sites dedicated to sports coverage. Good sports coverage also comes in highly specialised niche offerings online. Not only does the site feature traditional reporting and analysis, but a variety of interactive features allow golfers to get information customised to their game and interests. A variety of other local news providers have created important online sports news sites as well.

The news content on the internet has been evolving through three stages. In stage one, which still dominates many news sites, online journalists mostly just republish, or repurpose, content from their motherships. In stage two, which is gaining momentum and characterises most of the better news sites, the journalists create original content, augmenting it with such additives as hyperlinks to other websites; some interactive capabilities, such as search engines and electronic clickable indexes where the reader uses a mouse to select different content; some multimedia content, such as photos, video, and audio; and some customisation of sites and information, where readers create their one own personal news categories, stock listings, and other content. Stage three is only beginning to emerge, and only a handful of sites have attempted to enter it. This stage is characterised by original news content designed specifically for the web as a new medium of communication and frequently of increasingly specialised focus with full awareness and treatment of the internet as a legitimate medium of news delivery, a willingness to break news online aggressively and to rethink the nature of a community online, and, most importantly, a willingness to experiment with new forms of storytelling, such as immersive storytelling, which allows the reader to enter and navigate and throughout a news report rather than simply look at it in linear fashion, as is the case with traditional news reporting, still photography, motion video, and audio. Sometimes this storytelling is augmented with new technology.

News organisations and other content providers are committed to producing quality products. They know that young people are turning in growing numbers to online media. Research from a variety of sources since then confirms this trend and points to increasing use of the internet for news, especially among younger audiences. Moreover, these new digital tools are enabling news organisations to present their news in electronic formats increasingly accessible to people with disabilities.

Features of Web Journalism

The features that distinguish websites from other media are: multimedia, speed for updating information, horizontal distribution, decentralisation, accessibility, no hierarchy, no censorship and interactivity. Interactivity is the primary characteristic of new technologies and it has caused a considerable reassessment of communication research.Mass communication was originally modelled as the one-way transmission of a message from source to receiver. From Shannon and Weaver's model of communication, to the magic bullet theory, to the two-step flow model of media effects, to the principal of selective attention and perception, and finally the Westley and MacLean model, with its concepts of gatekeepers and feedback—all of these perspectives basically maintain a view of mass media as a one-way flow.

Interaction demands a two-way (or multi-directional) model of communication. With the interactive features of new media, the receiver is recognised as an active participant. People seek information or select information more than they "receive" information sent by journalists. To understand why and how people expose themselves to information, communi-cation scholars must consult selective exposure research rather than media effects research. At some websites, online readers can do more than actively select information— they also can add information. The distinction between source and receiver, therefore, is dissolving. Editors of online newspapers, however, may be wary of allowing users to become a source of mass communication messages.

Computers are interaction machines useful for communi-cating news. His position is based on a theory that both the needs of users and the nature of information are extremely fluid, sometimes changing from moment to moment. As an interactive device, a computer could communicate information about a constantly changing environment to the user, and it could provide a channel of communication from the user back to the news source. Such rapid feedback ensures practical news. With rapid feedback between equal communication "partners", the concept of a mass audience becomes archaic, even though mass production of messages does not. New media journalists cannot target a mass audience, defined as a large aggregate of undifferentiated yet hetero-geneous and anonymous people who are widely dispersed and not interactive. They cannot afford to take a distanced and undifferentiating view of the public. Now readers are linked to other readers directly, creating smaller, fragmented audiences who share much in common. They are a community rather than a mass audience, and research at the interpersonal level or the inter-group level may be more appropriate. If interactive features of online newspapers encourage a two-way (or multi-directional) flow of communication amongst a community of users, then the ritual model of communication seems more appropriate than the traditional transmission model. The ritual model is linked to such terms as sharing, participation, association, fellowship and the possession of a common faith. A ritual view is not directed towards the extension of messages in space, but the maintenance of society in time; not the act of imparting information but the representation of shared beliefs. Its emphasis is on the intrinsic satisfaction of the sender or receiver, rather than on some instrumental purpose. Like videotex companies, newspapers started online editions as a defensive marketing strategy. They seek to hold an audience's attention. Interactive devices, for example, are added to capture and hold an audience's attention. Interactive devices also are used to stimulate public discussions and draw thousands of people together in a virtual community. By listening to readers and involving them in news collection, online journalists attempt to increase reader satisfaction, leading to repeat visits. The publicity model, therefore, also applies to online papers. By holding people's attention, digital newspapers charging a subscription fee attain a direct economic goal, which is to gain audience revenue, and an indirect one, which is to sell the probability of audience attention to advertisers.

Interactive media designers must offer choices that have some meaning and consequence. At the same time, users must have an impact on the experience in some way. As users have greater effect upon the experience, they become more absorbed in the experience. What users do with content is more import-ant than how content may affect users. Users are actively chasing discovery, rather than passively being informed. Interactivity increases as:

i) the goal of communication is more to exchange information than to persuade participants have greater control of the communication environment.

ii) participants take an active role to fully benefit from the communication.

iii) participants act and react to messages via two-way communication.

iv) timing of communication is flexible and responsive to demands of participants.

v) communication environment creates a sense of place.

Online newspaper designers should realise that the more hyperlinks they add, the more choice users have to navigate through the newspaper site, and that these choices are important to interactivity. They should also understand that users are empowered when they can choose to use a text or graphics browser, or to receive information in English or a different language, or if they can use a search engine to find the information they want. Paisley defined interactivity mathematically as the ratio of user activity to system activity. At one extreme, users exert no effort beyond reading the text information which an online newspaper automatically pushes to them based upon information the users provided about themselves. At the other extreme, users select each page or screen to view, sending a message to the central computer asking to display the requested page.

Computer response is possible and ultimate machine interactivity is achieved when communication roles of human and machine are interchangeable. Such intelligent interactivity is currently difficult or impossible for media systems to achieve, but online newspapers can achieve lesser levels of responsive-ness by programming instructions, help pages and error messages. E-mail addresses can make communication easy between users and workers at online newspapers. Discussion forums and live chat areas attract and keep readers at a website. In addition, a site may offer synchronous communi-cation with data transfers occurring at fractions of a second, or at the other extreme, a mandatory time delay may be imposed, perhaps to allow editors to screen messages. Options concerning channels of communication, such as text, sound or full-motion video also can affect interpersonal communication. If online websites make it easy for users to add information, then they empower users. They stimulate creativity and discovery. Some online newspapers allow users to add the following types of information: web pages, hobby and special interest pages, announcements of births, marriages and deaths and reviews of movies, plays and other cultural and entertainment events.

News librarians and news researchers have spent considerable time in recent years training other journalists to do their own research. Reporters and others in the newsroom have scrambled to learn to use the web. General assignment and beat reporters, copy editors, investigative journalists and their editors have joined the online users list that has been headed by news researchers. Broadcast journalists also are using online research. Newsrooms have adopted personal computers as news gathering tools and as distribution media. Journalists also frequently go to the web to find government information. Furthermore, they seek background facts about businesses and they search for difficult-to-locate information, identify potential sources and use the information to improve depth and context in their coverage.

Before the beginning of commercial development of the web, online searching focused on the use of sophisticated commercial archives. The vastness of the internet has caused problems for journalists' ability to retrieve information with speed and efficiency. Locating US government information—the largest information gatherer in the world—has become increasingly difficult as agencies and departments place more information on the internet and reduce their production of paper-based documents. Finding the right statistics by using online resources is even more challenging because of their highly specific nature. The fluid nature of the internet and web may also cause problems. One authority on finding government information on the internet wrote that sites change their content, eliminate information, add information or reorganise it. This causes additional search problems. While there is a seemingly infinite amount of inexpensive information online, retrieving it is often frustrating and time consuming.

Web searching implies an organised process of determining what is needed and setting a strategy to find it. The growth of the web in recent years has forced even casual users to rethink their approaches and use search strategies and search tools in a more organised manner. The tools have evolved, resulting in constant change in their features and results. All of this also has modified how journalists find and retrieve information. Search engines permit users to find information contained in an indexed web search database. Search directory is a catalogue of documents presented by category and often involves user submission, editorial selection and editorial organisation. Search tools often vary in the basic user interface, which is the software employed to search at the basic and advanced levels.

Users must be aware that search outcomes may vary widely depending on the search engine's database size, the procedures used to develop the database, the frequency with which it is updated, the search options and the speed of response and user interface. Furthermore, there are differences in spiders, the software that searches the web, stores URLs and saves key words to build the database. Differences in these fundamental characteristics can produce different results. There are hundreds of search tools available. The number and variety of specialised search engines have also increased, focusing on news, multimedia, children, meta-searches and dozens of subjects. Journalists use both the search engine and search directory for finding information. For professional information searchers, the search tool used is not a matter of favourites or loyalties. Most authorities believe that search procedures are improving and becoming more user friendly. There are clearly more options and alternatives for searching, including advanced options.

The volume and complexity of finding information, as well as using search engines or directories may make users often frustrated. The common reaction is to give up and claim there is nothing available about the subject. Use of advanced search options, usually indicated by a hypertext link to a different page of the site, is one solution. Advanced searches help users by setting inclusive or exclusive dates, domain names or other types of search parameters.

Navigator and Internet Explorer have different default search sites, and journalists using the default settings likely will obtain different results from the same search instructions and key words. While Navigator once held market shares in the 80 and 90 per cent range, the share has slipped significantly in recent years as Internet Explorer has grown to dominate business and home browsing. Research during the past five years has shown journalists' browser use to be similar to that of other business users. Due to the success of well-established search tools used in databases such as Nexis-Lexis and Dialog, expectations of effectiveness of web search tools have often been high. However, the types of features, sophistication of software, reliability of features and reliability of the results are different from those of commercial services. Web tools are extensively used by professional information gatherers. Professional searchers employ a variety of strategies. Bates attributed the accomplishments of the best searchers to curiosity, use of an iterative or repetitive process, personal expertise and knowledge levels, analytical abilities, background discussions with clients and a sense of when to stop searching. Professionals include librarians, scholars, private investigators and some journalists who often spend large amounts of time online.

Web Blogs

A web blog is a website where entries are written in chronological order and commonly displayed in reverse chronological order. "Blog" can also be used as a verb, meaning to maintain or add content to a blog. Many blogs provide commentary or news on a particular subject such as food, politics, or local news; others function as more personal online diaries. A typical blog combines text, images, and links to other blogs, web pages, and other media related to its topic. The ability for readers to leave comments in an interactive format is an important part of many blogs. Most blogs are primarily textual, although some focus on art (artlog), photographs (photoblog), sketchblog, videos (vlog), music (MP3 blog), audio (podcasting) or sexual topics (Adult blog), and are part of a wider network of social media. Micro-blogging is another type of blogging which consists of blogs with very short posts.

Before blogging became popular, digital communities took many forms, including Usenet, commercial online services such as GEnie, BiX and the early CompuServe, e-mail lists and bulletin board systems (BBS). In the 1990s, Internet forum software, such as WebEx, created running conversations with "threads". Threads are topical connections between messages on a metaphorical "corkboard".

Usenet was the primary serial medium included in the original definition of the World Wide Web. It featured the Moderated Newsgroup which allowed all posting in a newsgroup to be under the control of an individual or small group. Most such newsgroups were simply moderated discussion forums, however, in 1983-84, one exception, named mod.ber, was created, named after and managed by an individual: Brian E. Redman. Regularly, Redman and a few associates posted summaries of interesting postings and threads taking place elsewhere on the net. With its serial journal publishing style, presence on the pre-HTTP web and strong similarity to the common blog form which features links to interesting and cool places on the net chosen by the blogger, mod.ber had many of the characteristics commonly associated with the term Blog. It ceased operation after approximately 8 months. Brad Templeton calls the newsgroup rec.humor.funny the world's oldest still existing blog.

The modern blog evolved from the online diary, where people would keep a running account of their personal lives. Most such writers called themselves diarists, journalists, or journalers. A few called themselves "escribitionists". The Open Pages webring included members of the online-journal community. Justin Hall, who began eleven years of personal blogging in 1994 while a student at Swarthmore College, is generally recognized as one of the earliest bloggers, as is Jerry Pournelle. Another early blog was Wearable Wireless Webcam, an online shared diary of a person's personal life combining text, video, and pictures transmitted live from a wearable computer and EyeTap device to a web site in 1994. This practice of semi-automated blogging with live video together with text, was referred to as sousveillance, and such journals were also used as evidence in legal matters.

Other forms of journals kept online also existed. A notable example was game programmer John Carmack's widely read journal, published via the finger protocol. Some of the very earliest bloggers, like Steve Gibson of sCary's Quakeholio (now Shacknews) and Stephen Heaslip of Blue's News (still running since 1995 with online archives back to July 1996), evolved from the Quake scene and Carmack's .plan updates. Steve Gibson was hired to blog full-time by Ritual Entertainment on February 8th, 1997 , possibly making him the first hired blogger.

Websites, including both corporate sites and personal homepages, had and still often have "What's New" or "News" sections, often on the index page and sorted by date. One example of a news based "weblog" is the Drudge Report founded by the self-styled maverick reporter Matt Drudge, though apparently Drudge dislikes this classification. Another is the Institute for Public Accuracy which began posting news releases featuring several news-pegged one-paragraph quotes several times a week beginning in 1998. One noteworthy early precursor to a blog was the tongue-in-cheek personal website that was frequently updated by Usenet legend Kibo.

Early weblogs were simply manually updated components of common websites. However, the evolution of tools to facilitate the production and maintenance of web articles posted in reverse chronological order made the publishing process feasible to a much larger, less technical, population. Ultimately, this resulted in the distinct class of online publishing that produces blogs we recognize today. For instance, the use of some sort of browser-based software is now a typical aspect of "blogging". Blogs can be hosted by dedicated blog hosting services, or they can be run using blog software, such as WordPress, Movable Type, blogger or LiveJournal, or on regular web hosting services, such as DreamHost.

The term "weblog" was coined by Jorn Barger on 17 December 1997. The short form, "blog," was coined by Peter Merholz, who jokingly broke the word weblog into the phrase we blog in the sidebar of his blog Peterme.com in April or May of 1999. This was quickly adopted as both a noun and verb ("to blog," meaning "to edit one's weblog or to post to one's weblog").

After a slow start, blogging rapidly gained in popularity. Blog usage spread during 1999 and the years following, being further popularized by the near-simultaneous arrival of the first hosted blog tools:

— Open Diary launched in October 1998, soon growing to thousands of online diaries. Open Diary innovated the reader comment, becoming the first blog community where readers could add comments to other writers' blog entries.

— Brad Fitzpatrick, a well known blogger started LiveJournal in March 1999.

— Andrew Smales created Pitas.com in July 1999 as an easier alternative to maintaining a "news page" on a website, followed by Diaryland in September 1999, focusing more on a personal diary community.

— Evan Williams and Meg Hourihan (Pyra Labs) launched blogger.com in August 1999.

Blogging combined the personal web page with tools to make linking to other pages easier - specifically permalinks, blogrolls and TrackBacks. This, together with weblog search engines enabled bloggers to track the threads that connected them to others with similar interests.

Several broadly popular American blogs emerged in 2001: Andrew Sullivan's AndrewSullivan.com, Ron Gunzburger's Politics1.com, Taegan Goddard's Political Wire, Glenn Reynolds' Instapundit, Charles Johnson's Little Green Footballs, and Jerome Armstrong's MyDD - all blogging primarily on politics.

By 2001, blogging was enough of a phenomenon that how-to manuals began to appear, primarily focusing on technique. The importance of the blogging community (and its relationship to larger society) increased rapidly. Established schools of journalism began researching blogging and noting the differences between journalism and blogging.

In 2002, Jerome Armstrong's friend and sometime business partner Markos Moulitsas Zúniga began DailyKos. With up to a million visits a day during peak events, it has now become one of the Internet's most popular blogs. Also in 2002, many blogs focused on comments by U.S. Senate Majority Leader Trent Lott. Senator Lott, at a party honoring U.S. Senator Strom Thurmond, praised Senator Thurmond by suggesting that the United States would have been better off had Thurmond been elected president. Lott's critics saw these comments as a tacit approval of racial segregation, a policy advocated by Thurmond's 1948 presidential campaign. This view was reinforced by documents and recorded interviews dug up by bloggers. Though Lott's comments were made at a public event attended by the media, no major media organizations reported on his controversial comments until after blogs broke the story. Blogging helped to create a political crisis that forced Lott to step down as majority leader.

The impact of this story gave greater credibility to blogs as a medium of news dissemination. Though often seen as partisan gossips, bloggers sometimes lead the way in bringing key information to public light, with mainstream media having to follow their lead. More often, however, news blogs tend to react to material already published by the mainstream media. Since 2002, blogs have gained increasing notice and coverage for their role in breaking, shaping, and spinning news stories. The Iraq war saw bloggers taking measured and passionate points of view that go beyond the traditional left-right divide of the political spectrum. Blogging by established politicians and political candidates, to express opinions on war and other issues, cemented blogs' role as a news source. Meanwhile, an increasing number of experts blogged, making blogs a source of in-depth analysis.

The second Iraq war was the first "blog war" in another way: Iraqi bloggers gained wide readership, and one, Salam Pax, published a book of his blog. Blogs were also created by soldiers serving in the Iraq war. Such "warblogs" gave readers new perspectives on the realities of war, as well as often offering different viewpoints from those of official news sources.

Blogging was used to draw attention to obscure news sources. For example, bloggers posted links to traffic cameras in Madrid as a huge anti-terrorism demonstration filled the streets in the wake of the March 11 attacks.

Bloggers began to provide nearly-instant commentary on televised events, creating a secondary meaning of the word "blogging": to simultaneously transcribe and editorialize speeches and events shown on television. Real-time commentary is sometimes referred to as "liveblogging."

In 2004, the role of blogs became increasingly mainstream, as political consultants, news services and candidates began using them as tools for outreach and opinion forming. Even politicians not actively campaigning, such as the UK's Labour Party's MP Tom Watson, began to blog to bond with constituents.

Minnesota Public Radio broadcast a program by Christopher Lydon and Matt Stoller called "The blogging of the President," which covered a transformation in politics that blogging seemed to presage. The Columbia Journalism Review began regular coverage of blogs and blogging. Anthologies of blog pieces reached print, and blogging personalities began appearing on radio and television. In the summer of 2004, both United States Democratic and Republican Parties' conventions credentialed bloggers, and blogs became a standard part of the publicity arsenal. Mainstream television programs, such as Chris Matthews' Hardball, formed their own blogs. Merriam-Webster's Dictionary declared "blog" as the word of the year in 2004.

In 2004, Global Voices Online, a site which "aggregates, curates, and amplifies the global conversation online - shining light on places and people other media often ignore" surfaced, bringing to light bloggers from around the world. Today, the site has a relationship with Reuters and is responsible for breaking many global news stories.

Blogs were among the driving forces behind the "Rathergate" scandal, to wit: (television journalist) Dan Rather presented documents (on the CBS show 60 Minutes) that conflicted with accepted accounts of President Bush's military service record. Bloggers declared the documents to be forgeries and presented evidence and arguments in support of that view, and CBS apologized for what it said were inadequate reporting techniques. Many bloggers view this scandal as the advent of blogs' acceptance by the mass media, both as a news source and opinion and as means of applying political pressure.

Some bloggers have moved over to other media. The following bloggers (and others) have appeared on radio and television: Duncan Black (known widely by his pseudonym, Atrios), Glenn Reynolds (Instapundit), Markos Moulitsas Zúniga (Daily Kos), Alex Steffen (Worldchanging) and Ana Marie Cox (Wonkette). In counter-point, Hugh Hewitt exemplifies a mass media personality who has moved in the other direction, adding to his reach in "old media" by being an influential blogger.

Some blogs were an important news source during the December 2004 Tsunami such as Medecins Sans Frontieres, which used SMS text messaging to report from affected areas in Sri Lanka and Southern India. Similarly, during Hurricane Katrina in August 2005 and the aftermath a few blogs which were located in New Orleans, including the Interdictor and Gulfsails were able to maintain power and an Internet connection and disseminate information that was not covered by the Main Stream Media.

In the United Kingdom, The Guardian newspaper launched a redesign in September 2005, which included a daily digest of blogs on page 2. Also in June 2006, BBC News launched a weblog for its editors, following other news companies. In January 2005, Fortune magazine listed eight bloggers that business people "could not ignore": Peter Rojas, Xeni Jardin, Ben Trott, Mena Trott, Jonathan Schwartz, Jason Goldman, Robert Scoble, and Jason Calacanis.

Popularity of Blogs

Recently, researchers have analyzed the dynamics of how blogs become popular. There are essentially two measures of this: popularity through citations, as well as popularity through affiliation (i.e. blogroll). The basic conclusion from studies of the structure of blogs is that while it takes time for a blog to become popular through blogrolls, permalinks can boost popularity more quickly, and are perhaps more indicative of popularity and authority than blogrolls, since they denote that people are actually reading the blog's content and deem it valuable or noteworthy in specific cases.

Recently, through the mass popularity of sponsored post ventures such as PayPerPost a massive amount of personal blogs have started writing sponsored posts for advertisers wanting to boost buzz about new products and services. It has revolutionised the blogosphere almost in the same way that Google AdSense did.

The blogdex project was launched by researchers in the MIT Media Lab to crawl the Web and gather data from thousands of blogs in order to investigate their social properties. It gathered this information for over 4 years, and autonomously tracked the most contagious information spreading in the blog community, ranking it by recency and popularity. It can thus be considered the first instantiation of a memetracker. The project is no longer active, but a similar function is now served by tailrank.com.

Blogs are also given rankings by Technorati based on the amount of incoming links and Alexa Internet based on the web hits of Alexa Toolbar users. In August 2006, Technorati listed the most linked-to blog as that of Chinese actress Xu Jinglei and the most-read blog as group-written Boing Boing.

Gartner forecasts that blogging will peak in 2007, leveling off when the number of writers who maintain a personal website reaches 100 million. Gartner analysts expect that the novelty value of the medium will wear off as most people who are interested in the phenomenon have checked it out, and new bloggers will offset the number of writers who abandon their creation out of boredom. The firm estimates that there are more than 200 million former bloggers who have ceased posting to their online diaries, creating an exponential rise in the amount of "dotsam" and "netsam" - that is to say, unwanted objects on the Web.

It was reported by Chinese media Xinhua that the blog of Xu Jinglei received more than 50 million page views, claiming to be the most popular blog in the world.

In mid-2006, it also had the most incoming links of any blogs on the Internet.

Blog as Mass Media

Many bloggers, particularly those engaged in participatory journalism, differentiate themselves from the mainstream media, while others are members of that media working through a different channel. Some institutions see blogging as a means of "getting around the filter" and pushing messages directly to the public. Some critics worry that bloggers respect neither copyright nor the role of the mass media in presenting society with credible news. Bloggers and other contributors to user generated content are behind Time magazine naming their 2006 person of the year as "you".

Many mainstream journalists, meanwhile, write their own blogs - well over 300, according to CyberJournalist.net's J-blog list. The first known use of a weblog on a news site was in August 1998, when Jonathan Dube of The Charlotte Observer published one chronicling Hurricane Bonnie.

Blogs have also had an influence on minority languages, bringing together scattered speakers and learners; this is particularly so with blogs in Gaelic languages, whose creators can be found as far away from traditional Gaelic areas as Kazakhstan and Alaska. Minority language publishing (which may lack economic feasibility) can find its audience through inexpensive blogging.

There are many examples of bloggers who have published books based on their blogs, e.g., Salam Pax, Ellen Simonetti, Jessica Cutler. Blog-based books have been given the name blook. Indeed, a prize for the best blog-based book was initiated in 2005, The Lulu Blooker Prize.

Although success has been elusive offline, with many of these books not selling as well as their blogs. Only sex blogger Tucker Max cracked the New York Time's Bestseller List.

The emergence of blogging has brought a range of legal liabilities and other often unforeseen consequences. One area of concern is the issue of bloggers releasing proprietary or confidential information. Another area of concern is blogging and defamation. A third area of concern is employees who write about aspects of their place of employment or their personal lives, and then face loss of employment or other adverse consequences.

Ethical Issues in Web Journalism

Many news organisations that have launched online efforts now operate and staff their web operations separately from their traditional newsrooms. Consider the case of newspaper sites that feature book reviews linked to online booksellers, such as *Amazon.com* or *bn.com* These newspapers receive a commission when a reader buys a book the news site has reviewed. Very few news sites reveal this to the reader, or, if they do publish this information, it is often buried deep in the site. Today's internet and World Wide Web make it possible for nearly everyone to own an electronic press. For online content providers, especially news providers, it raises difficult questions about the blurring boundary between advertising and editorial content online. But many traditional news organisations that own a press have a commitment to act responsibly; they view their work as part of a public trust. Those who operate a licensed broadcast operation have a legal obligation to serve in the public interest.

It is incumbent upon schools and departments of journalism to play an active role in educating the public to act responsibly in creating electronic content and in assuming a leadership role in shaping public behaviours on the net. The issue of who is a journalist in the digital age also raises what is perhaps the most vexing ethical question facing journalism today. Increasingly, many argue that objectivity, fairness, and accuracy are not only problematic but may in fact be fostering irresponsibility by limiting the accountability of the reporter to the truthfulness of what he reports. In other words, the journalist can hide behind the cloak of objectivity, fairness, and accuracy, without addressing the more fundamental issue of whether what he has reported is actually true. The rise of online journalism transforms this issue. As new sources of news emerge and as the public turns to an ever-widening array of news sources, the practices and standards of those diverse sources is increasingly uncertain. Perhaps by moving outside the ideology of objectivity, these alternative news sources may help to put the facts into a more complete context and perspective.

For more than a century, members of the press have been obsessed with the notion that a reporter must make his or her deadline. In other words, a story turned in past deadline is virtually worthless. There are several reasons, including the belief that by not making a deadline, a journalist is not acting professionally or not working hard enough. Another important reason is the belief that missing a deadline, especially on breaking news, means that a competitor will likely get the story first. Newspapers require reporters to make certain closing times in order to make their print runs and be on the delivery truck or in the newsstands in time for the morning rush hour. As a result of this technical requirement, newspapers and other news media, have developed an obsession with making their deadlines. The requirements of analog television, especially with timed broadcasts, reinforce this orientation. Frequently, deadline pressures have serious negative consequences for the truthfulness of the news. Journalists under intense deadline pressure can make errors, sometimes serious ones, have little time for fact checking, and can even get a story fundamentally wrong, all for the sake of making a deadline. Sources may not be reached for comment because of the need to make a deadline. News organisations less obsessed with deadlines might very well be better at getting a story right, although they might sometimes sacrifice getting the story first.

Although some critics contend that new media, because of the instantaneous quality of the online world, suffer the ill effects of speed even more than their traditional analog counterparts, the reality is somewhat more complex. Online news organisations, especially those that are original to the internet, in reality have no particular deadline, or, rather, they face a continuous deadline: their deadlines are totally self-imposed. Of course, when news is breaking, the pressure is now even more intense to get the story before any of a thousand competitors. But on just about any story after day one, online news providers can take as much time as they feel necessary to get the story right before posting it online. By freeing journalists from the artificial, technologically induced deadline delirium of twentieth-century journalism, the digital age may usher in an era of journalism dominated less by the clock and more by the need to get the facts right.

Questions that frame the ethical issues, mainly come from the areas of news-gathering. Consider the case of a journalist equipped with an omnidirectional video camera. He could use it to present dynamic events in a compelling immersive environment and to help put stories in better context. But an omnicamera means more than just better news gathering. It raises serious ethical concerns as well. For one thing, omnidirectional video can place everyone at a scene under surveillance, whether the camera is pointed at them or not. These possible developments have the potential to erode the credibility of the media/ journalism even further. One hundred fifty years of photography have taught people to understand that they are being watched when a camera lens is pointed at them. But a single-lens omnicamera shoots video by pointing the lens at a parabolic mirror, which means one is being watched even when the omnicamera is pointing away. Further, when watching conventional video, the viewer does not have control over what he is watching. Since omnivideo is digital, the viewer has full control over the video, including the ability to pan, tilt, and zoom. This means the viewer may use the video in ways the journalist never intended. Hidden cameras raise many of the sane issues. Undercover and investigative reporting aided by a variety of new media applications may increasingly invade people's privacy. The use of remote sensing technology offers unobstructed views from space of individuals at home in their backyards.

Traditionally journalists have been among the heaviest users of such public records. They have fought valiantly to protect and expand access to such records, arguing that freedom of expression has little meaning if access to information is not guaranteed. In US when, APB news made its request for the records of all 1,600 federal judges, they were denied access. The argument was that releasing such information on the internet would threaten the safety of the judges and their families.

APBnews argued in its legal challenge to this decision that its FOIA request was just as protected by law as that of a newspaper. The records themselves do not provide information that identifies family members, and, if they did, this information could be deleted before posting the records online. The public has a right to know if a judge has a financial conflict of interest in a case, and only these records would reveal the truth. In 2000, APBnews won this case, and it may help define freedom of speech in the digital world and the ethical limits of a responsible online press. Journalists and the public need access to public records and records of governmental transactions in order to check on government activities and uncover potential abuse. This is often called the watchdog function of the press, the reason the press is often described as the fourth estate or the fourth branch of government. Yet in a digital age the nature of information and what can be done with it changes dramatically.

Availability of late-received digital video raises what is perhaps the biggest concern in the era of the digital newsroom: the veracity of video received from an increasingly diverse array of digital sources. When news footage arrived in the newsroom in canisters of 16 or 35 mm film, it was relatively easy to confirm the accuracy of the content received: the film negative established the authenticity of the images. Even in the days of exclusively analog video a producer could be reasonably confident that images had not been manipulated since being recorded on tape. In the old-fashioned analog television newsroom, it took an entire team of reporters, editors, and union technicians to gather, edit, and put on the air a single piece of video. Many pairs of eyes routinely viewed every video clip that made it on to the air. In the digital video newsroom, the number of eyes and concomitant amount of experience reviewing any given video is greatly reduced, not just for technical reasons but for reasons of cost cutting.

Today, digital technologies make it possible to change the aspect ratio or any other dimension of even moving images and to do so seamlessly so that no viewer can tell the images have been manipulated. Digital image manipulation comes in three basic forms: addition, substruction, and modification. Digital addition refers to putting something into a picture that was not originally there, such as a crowd at a football stadium. Digital subtraction refers to removing something from a picture, such as deleting someone or something, such as a cable supporting an actor who appears to be flying. Digital manipulation means transforming an image, such as making it lighter or darker. As a result of the advent of digital image processing and potenti-ally manipulation in the television newsroom, the traditional value of verifying any news content through multiple reliable sources is more critical than ever. In the age of the digital newsroom and the information super-highway, news organisations will need to be vigilant in their pursuit of reliable news video, digital or not. Digital technologies have magnified the traditional ethical issues surrounding news production. Although it has always been possible for darkroom technicians to manipulate images, digital technologies make such manipulation easier than ever and much harder to detect. Aside from alterations such as those described above, it is now possible to use such technology to create completely synthetic moving pictures, or video, as well as sound. It is relatively easy and inexpensive to use what are called nonlinear digital video editors.

Although the ethical issues of image and sound manipulation may not be new the dramatic impact of digital technology has magnified the problem. It is now possible for even those with limited training and resources to create completely synthetic still or moving images and transmit them via the internet to a global audience, perhaps on the eve of an important election, possibly exerting a dramatic impact on the outcome of a close vote. Bringing this issue closer to home, the broadcast networks in 1999 began embracing new digital imaging technologies. Networks such as CBS, ABC, Fox, and ESPN have begun using these technologies extensively to place virtual logos in programmes such as CBS's The Early Show or to place a yellow line on the football field during the National Football League games to indicate the so-called first down marker. Although these tools are highly effective in a commercial sense, their use has come under some heavy criticism when used in news programming as being an unethical manipulation of reality. Radio broadcasters have also employed the new digital tools. One particularly interesting technology is called time compression or, in the industry vernacular, simply cash, for the money it makes. This technology enables radio broadcasters to speed up recorded or even live programmes ever so slightly—unnoticeably to the listener—by compressing pauses and thereby have room to insert eight additional 30-second commercials into each programme hour. Again, this is highly desirable commercially but has been criticised as inappropriate ethically.

Today, there is no industrywide standards define the level of image or sound alteration that is acceptable within the boundaries of ethical journalism. On one end of the spectrum, there is universal agreement that it is permissible to crop pictures or edit actualities, although not to change a speaker's meaning. On the other end of the spectrum, all journalists agree that creating completely synthetic news events is unethical. It is the great gray area in between where there is no consensus. In fields such as advertising, digital image manipulation is the *de facto* standard, yet the public might still be surprised by the lengths to which it is done. Should the public learn how widespread digital image manipulation is confidence in all the media, journalism included, will likely fall, unless journalism as a whole adopts a universal code of digital ethics.

Another major ethical concern for news organisations is the real or perceived potential conflicts of interest reporters or news organisations might have that would prevent them from covering a news story fairly or objectively. A major potential conflict of interest faces many online news providers involved in covering the world's increasingly electronic financial markets. In contrast to the analog media and investment worlds, the digital age has brought real-time stock quotes, data, and online trading capabilities to virtually everyone with a computer and a modem. Day traders, as they are called, as well as computer-automated trading programmes, make split-second decisions based on narrow decision rules and newly acquired information that they think may give them a slight, short-lived market advantage.

Many websites already track generalised patterns of visitor behaviour. Targeting technologies go a step further by creating custom profiles of every surfer who visits a site from a particular computer. Most often, the website does not know who you are, but it does know something about your surfing and buying behaviours. Over time, it can smooth your browsing experience so you can find the editorial content you want more quickly, and it can make pretty good guesses about the kinds of ads you might welcome—and place them on your screen instantly. Online companies have begun sharing data about consumer buying and browsing habits, and some have even matched that data against direct marketing mailing lists to discover users' identities and track their buying habits.

Every day we read about ethical lapses fostered in cyber-space: the stealth drug company site masquerading as a health information centre, misleading stock tips made in financial chat rooms, electronic shopping bots whose results are skewed to favour retail clients, e-commerce sites' egregious violations of users' privacy. Compared to this sorry track record, online news sites have performed admirably. That is not to say that journalism on the web has been flawless. Both traditional news operations and newcomers like Slate and Salon have encountered their fair share of ethical controversies. Online journalism ethics might be grouped into three broad categories:

i) *Gathering the news*: Journalists face a new host of ethical considerations related to the online medium, ranging from a reporter concealing her identity in a chat room to quoting from bulletin board postings to recording and streaming digital footage without the subject's permission.

ii) *Reporting the news*: Speed is one of the internet's greatest virtues and vices. In the current saturated media environment, the internet heightens the intense com-petitive pressures to be first while a story is still developing and key facts remain unknown. Is there a looser standard for reporting in a medium where infor-mation wants to be free and where speed reigns supreme?

iii) *Presenting the news*: While print publications have long been governed by an implicit separation of church and state, the line between editorial and business interests is often blurred in a web universe where the main rule is to survive. Online editorial staffers face questions about their web sites' ad placement, the influence of e-commerce on editorial decisions, and related questions that affect credibility and editorial independence.

Online news gathering has enhanced rather than detracted from journalism's credibility. The online medium gives journalists the powerful tools of context and authentication. Reporters and editors use the net's links-based architecture to provide users with important background information, resources and archived articles that allow users to glimpse the trajectory of a news story over time. Equally important is the ability to link to source materials, transcripts, public records and other original documents to buttress an article's reporting. In this age of public mistrust of the media, such steps enhance a news organisation's credibility. News gathering techniques on the net do present some new challenges for journalists. If your gut tells you that you are heading into ethically gray territory, consult with other journalists but also with non-journalists who may be better steeped in the hallowed tradition of netiquette, or acceptable behaviour online.

The decade ahead promises to thrust online news gathering techniques into the spotlight far more prominently as untold thousands of net users take on the mantle of amateur reporters and begin lone-wolf operations to cover stories in their back yards and neighborhoods, complete with weblogs and video footage online but absent the standards of professional newsrooms. People want information faster than they did ever before. The news cycle seems a quaint idea when stories can erupt, spread and die in a matter of hours. Much of the concern about the internet's impact on journalism centres on the new medium's emphasis on speed and immediacy, which properly remain central tenets of online publishing. Not long ago, news sites were content to publish only stories from the morning paper. For most large and mid-sized online newspapers, those days are thankfully gone, as users demand timely details about news events as they occur. Millions of us flock to our computer screens for the latest developments whenever a big story hits.

The challenge facing online journalists is to balance the legitimate desires of the online audience for up-to-the-minute reports with the profession's traditions of fairness, complete-ness, balance and accuracy. There's an inherent tension built into such an equation, but instantaneous reporting is a skill set mastered long ago by wire service reporters and by television and radio news professionals covering live events. Online news sites that continually update their breaking-news reports with new information have generally done a good job in bringing bulletins to the masses. But sometimes competitive pressures win out. While newspapers and broadcasters abide by traditions governing the separation of editorial and advertising, and trade association guidelines establish rules for the display of ads and advertorials, and publications have adopted standards covering conflicts of interest and the like, few such rules have very deep roots on the Web. *The New York Times* was roundly criticised by journalism academics in 1998 when it began offering a link to barnesandnoble.com on its website's books pages. In recent years other online publications, such as washingtonpost.com, have entered the e-commerce marketplace, selling goods on its Website. All these efforts bear close scrutiny to ensure that editorial decisions are not influenced by financial consider-ations, just as has long been the case in print newsrooms. Other news sites, such as CNET's News.com, earlier this year began running oversized ads smack in the middle of editorial copy in an effort to induce users to click on them. Other online news sites are expected to follow suit in the coming months. Online publishers need to do more work to ensure that users do not become confused by the intrusion of commercial content into the editorial space.

Over the past few years, online journalists have taken some hard knocks and learned some tough lessons. While press coverage has cast blame on 'the internet' for many of journalism's sins and shortcomings, perhaps a little perspective is in order. Only three years ago, the journalism world shuddered at the prospect that Matt Drudge was chiselling the new rules of the road for internet reporting. At conferences, in newsrooms and at corner taverns, reporters bemoaned a world in which a celebrated purveyor of rumour and innuendo plied his trade without bothering to verify the allegations he zapped off into cyberspace each day. Others wondered whether traditional journalism had a home in a medium in which speed was often valued above verification, where first-person diatribes trumped balanced reporting, where noise crowded out signal. Today, net has came to the mainstream. In USA alone, it has over 100 million adults now online, compared with about half that number three years ago, the internet now much more closely reflects society's values. The principles and values that matter to Americans in print and broadcast news—fairness, accuracy, balance, even-handedness—also matter to them in the online medium. In April, MSNBC appointed the first ombudsman of an online news organisation: Dan Fisher, a respected former editor and foreign bureau chief at the *Los Angeles Times*. The online papers get greater credence than the print media because these news operations have transferred their greatest assets —their credibility and trustworthiness— to the online medium, while at the same time taking advantage of some of the net's key assets: its nonlinear nature; its instantaneity and convenience; its authentication value; and its interactivity.

Bibliography

Alberts, D.S., and D.S. Papp, (eds.) 1997. *The Information Age· An Anthology on Its Impact and Consequences.* Washington, DC: National Defense University.

Allen, T., and M.S. Morton, (eds.) 1994. *Information Technology and the Corporation of the 1990s.* New York: Oxford University Press.

Ante, S.E., with A. Borrus and R.D. Hof. 2001. "In Search of the Net's Next Big Thing." *Business Week* (March 26): 141.

Berners-Lee, Tim, et.al., (December 15, 2004). "*Architecture of the World Wide Web, Volume One*". Version 20041215. W3C.

Brunnel, D. 2000. *Making the Cisco Connection: The Story Behind the Real Internet Superpower.* New York: John Wiley.

Castells, M. 1996. *The Rise of the Network Society.* Cambridge, MA: Basil Blackwell.

Clemente, P.C. 1998. *State of the Net: The New Frontier.* New York: McGraw-Hill.

Cyert, R., and D. Mowery, (eds.) 1987. *Technology and Employment: Innovation and Growth in the U.S. Economy.* Washington, DC: National Academy Press.

Danziger, J.N., and K.L. Kraemer. 1986. *People and Computers: The Impacts of Computing on End Users in Organizations.* New York: Columbia University Press.

Drucker, P.F. 1999. "Beyond the Information Revolution." Atlantic Monthly 284 (4/October): 47–57.

Fielding, R., et al.,. (June 1999). "*Hypertext Transfer Protocol — HTTP/ 1.1*". Request For Comments 2616. Information Sciences Institute.

Forester, T. 1989. *Computers in the Human Context: Information Technology, Productivity, and People.* Cambridge, MA: MIT Press.

Katz, L.F. 2000. "Technological Change, Computerization, and the Wage Structure." In E. Brynjolfsson and B. Kahin, eds. *Understanding the Digital Economy.* Cambridge, MA: MIT Press.

Khosrowpour, M. 1994. *Information Technology and Organizations: Challenges of New Technologies.* Harrisburg, PA: Idea Group Publishing.

Kranzberg, M. 1989. "IT as Revolution." In T. Forester, ed., *Computers in the Human Context: Information Technology, Productivity, and People.* Cambridge, MA: MIT Press.

Lawrence, S., and L. Giles. 1999. "Accessibility of Information on the Web." *Nature* 400 (July 8): 107–09.

Lerner, J., and J. Tirole. 2001. "The Open Source Movement: Key Research Questions." *European Economic Review* 45: 819–26.

Office of Technology Assessment (OTA). 1995. *Teachers and Technology: Making the Connection.* Washington, DC: U.S. Government Printing Office.

Polo, Luciano (2003). World Wide Web Technology Architecture: A Conceptual Analysis. *New Devices.* Retrieved on July 31, 2005.

Wong, R., and R. Jesty. 2001. "The Wireless Internet: Applications, Technology and Market Strategies." Available at http://www.allnetdevices.com/wireless/opinions/2001/01/10/the_wireless.html. Accessed September 17, 2001.

World Information Technology and Services Alliance. 1999. *Digital Planet: The Global Information Economy.* Arlington, VA: WITSA.

Index